CAVE PHOT
A Practic

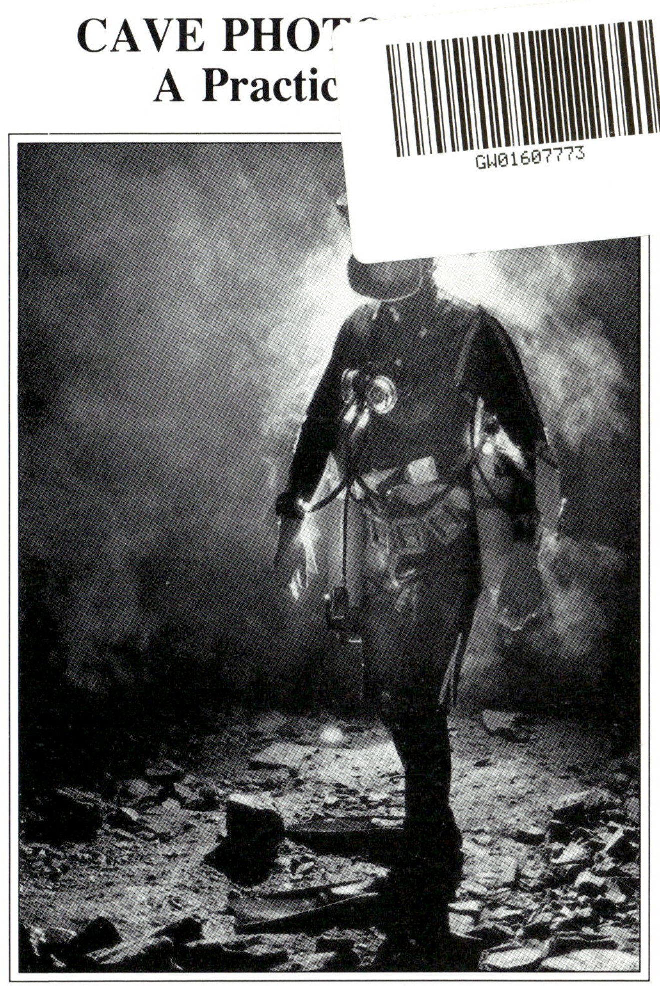

Chris Howes

Published by Caving Supplies, Buxton

Acknowledgements

The photographs in this book could only have been taken with the aid of my friends. To name everybody would be a major task, and I hope I will be forgiven for any omissions from the following list, to whom I extend my gratitude. Featured in the pictures are; Mike Baines, Rod Beaumont, Peter Bolt, Alan Calford, Judith Calford, John Cliffe, Pete Cloke, Tim Fewster, Chris Hurley, Ruth Jacobs, Andy Kendal, Steve Kings, Tony Knibbs, Jane Mitchell, Gavin Newman, Simon Raven, Hugh Rice, Phil Sandercott, Theo Schuurmans, Tom Sharpe, Richard Stevenson and Pete Watkinson.

A special mention must be made of the following. First, Martyn Farr, who first suggested that I write this book, and kept encouraging me to do so. Rod 'Bomber' Beaumont, for presenting me with my first slave unit, and Andy Bell for his many hours designing my infra-red version, exceeding all my criteria whilst he did so. Lastly, Judith Calford for continuing to tolerate me underground as well as above whilst this volume was produced.

Without the aid of these cavers none of my projects could have been realised. This book is therefore dedicated to my many cold, wet, willing (and unwilling) friends who suffered in the cause of cave photography. And thank you.

Chris Howes
Cardiff, June 1987

The majority of the photographs in this book have been taken on a Rollei 35 LED or Olympus OM2n with a 50mm or 28-48mm zoom lens. Most colour pictures are on Ektachrome 200. Black and white were shot on Ilford FP4 and developed in Paterson's Acutol or Kodak HC110. Prints were made on Kentmere glossy resin-coated paper.

Front Cover: Gavin Newman, Ogof Ffynnon Ddu. E2, B5.
Back Cover: Phil Sandercott, Dan yr Ogof. E1, B5.
Title Page: Rod Beaumont, Silica Mines, Glyn Neath. Fixed light 8, E5.

First published in 1987 by Caving Supplies, 19 London Road, Buxton, Derbyshire, SK17 9PA.
Printed in Great Britain by Trio Graphics Ltd., Gloucester.
Photographs laser scanned for high quality reproduction.

British Library Cataloguing in Publication Data.

HOWES, Chris
Cave Photography: a practical guide.
1. Photography of caves
I. Title
778.9'9551447 TR788

ISBN 0-9512204-0-3

CONTENTS

Introduction

1. Equipment.
Cameras, lenses, flashguns, batteries, slave units, tripod, cable release, film.

2. Preparations.
Cameras, electronic flash, bulb flash, slave units, ammunition box and transport, tripods, insurance, packing, cleaning.

3. Using A Single Flash.
Using the 'B' setting, advantages of slave units, placing lights, bulbs or electronic flash, determining the aperture to use.

4. Multiple Flash.
Using the 'B' setting, placing flashguns, obtaining even lighting, adding backlighting, bulb and electronic flash combinations.

Conclusion

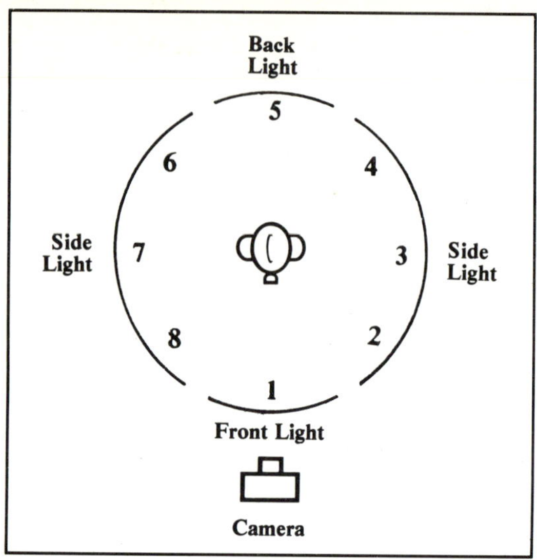

Lighting Positions

Photographs in this guide have been chosen to illustrate various lighting positions and angles of illumination. The basic flashgun positions relative to the subject from the camera position are shown in this diagram. Bulbs are indicated by a letter 'B', electronic flash by 'E'. Thus, this photograph in ***Kingsdale Master Cave*** *produced with B5, E2 has a bulb used for backlight and an electronic flash to add detail from the front.*

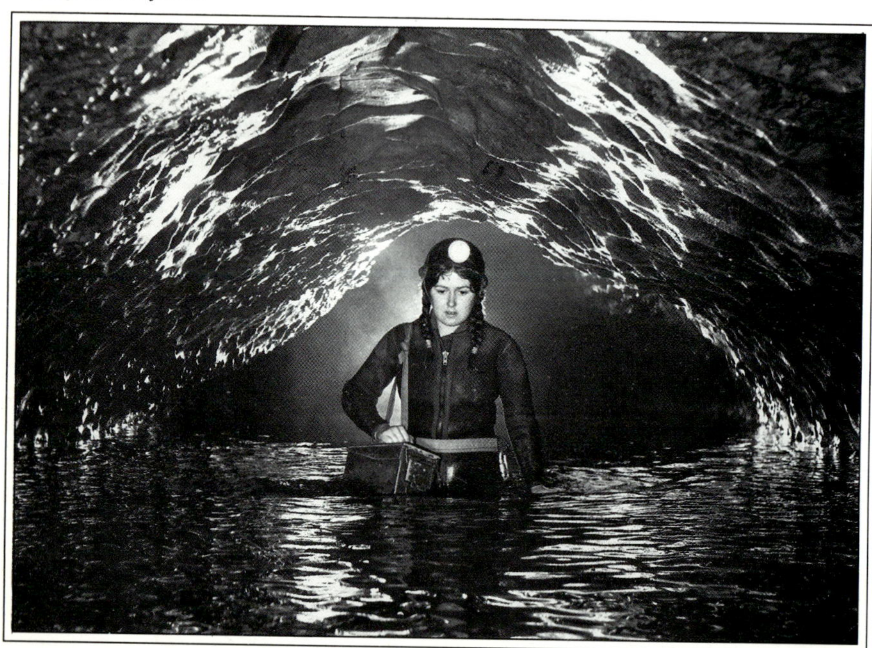

INTRODUCTION

It is hard to imagine anything more hostile to photography than a cave environment. Dirt, mud, grit, high humidity and water, all conspire to ensure that every attempt to produce a photograph will end in failure - not just of the picture but eventually of the camera and flashguns as well. Frequently, the final result is a bland, poorly exposed misty print or transparency that lacks depth or atmosphere.

Yet, the number of cavers setting out to produce their own photographs, despite the difficulties, continues to increase. This book is aimed at these people. The theory behind the various techniques at their command is discussed, but the emphasis is on the practical production of pictures in a successful way.

Whether you are primarily photographer or caver, by using the suggestions in this book you can avoid some of the pitfalls which are not always obvious to those without experience, and you will raise the success rate and quality of your pictures. If you have ever wondered how to determine exposures when operating five flashguns, or are uncertain why the results you have produced are inconsistent and just aren't what you wanted, then this guide is for you.

The novice photographer will find plenty of advice within these pages, but there is an equal wealth of information for those already involved with recording caves or mines on film. There are many techniques and methods that can be used to tackle photography underground. Different cavers use different approaches. It is important to consider how to develop techniques and specialist equipment that suit you, and which will help produce an individual style of your own.

It is for this reason that this book is a 'guide'. It can be used as a 'how-to-do-it recipe book' to produce a picture by following the instructions, but never be scared to change and modify the techniques in this guide to suit yourself. The system described here is not the only one in existence, but it is both simple and effective. Elements within it may not suit you personally, and may require altering to suit your own equipment and ideas. If you think of a way round a problem, then try it out! But walk before you run, and make sure that you understand the basic techniques included in these pages before you do. It will save you time in the long run.

The adage 'Leave nothing but footprints, kill nothing but time, take nothing but photographs' is an important one. A cave is a delicate place, easily damaged by a stray foot whilst you set up a photograph. Never risk a fragile formation for the sake of a picture. Take care, and pictures which fulfil your desire to record this special environment may be made in an enjoyable way. Above all, that is what counts.

1

EQUIPMENT

Cameras

Many of the problems of cave photography that arise underground can be avoided or minimised by the correct choice of camera, flashguns, and associated equipment. Of these, the most basic is the camera itself.

If you already own a camera you may not wish to consider purchasing another specifically for cave photography, although this course of action has much to commend it. If your main camera is an expensive automatic model, there is little point in subjecting it to the rigours it will have to undergo once below ground. Give some serious thought to keeping one camera bought specially for underground use, and another for general work and holiday pictures. There is no need to spend a fortune at this stage, and second hand models are a distinct possibility. Once you have developed your technique you can always upgrade to a better 35mm or medium format camera, if you wish. Any camera can be used, but some are far more suitable than others. Obviously, anything that is fragile or that has small gaps which can easily admit water, mud or dirt into the mechanism has to be ruled out. It is impossible to comment on every individual camera on the market, there are just too many of them. But some general features are useful, some are useless, and some are to be avoided. As a first step, decide on the format.

For any serious underground photography, film such as 110 and disc format has to be ruled out. These are the smallest formats generally available, and are used in cameras such as the Instamatic. Although capable of being used in caves, they are too limiting for general photography. There is poor control over aperture, shutter speed, and the way that flashguns are attached, and the negative is too small to allow adequate quality of enlargements. Instant picture cameras, such as Polaroid, are likewise of limited use (although you might wish to use one to check an important shot before taking the final version on film). If you want a quick record of the results of a dig or your mates in action the integral flash might suffice, but otherwise it is too weak and close to the lens to permit much control. Overall, although all these formats and cameras are cheap and light, better models may be found for underground work.

Medium format cameras use roll film, and give a much larger negative which permits better quality of reproduction. However, both twin lens and single lens medium format reflex cameras are large (usually one fills a double ammunition box on it's own), heavy, and phenomenally expensive. If you are taking photographs for use as posters or book illustrations the publisher may require this size of film, leaving you with no choice, but unless you have a specific purpose in mind these cameras are not needed by the average caver.

This leaves the 35mm camera as the best choice. These are generally cheaper, the choice is vast, and there is the possibility of buying second hand. The pictures in this book were taken on a variety of cameras, but all are 35mm format. Whatever you decide upon, the ideal caving camera (not that there is such a thing!) should possess as many of the following features as possible.

The lens quality should be as good as you can afford, since it is upon this that the crispness and contrast of the finished picture will depend. You will need control over the aperture in use, thus ruling out any of the totally automatic compact models. Likewise, you will need to be able to select a shutter speed manually. This must be 1/30th of a second or slower to use with flashbulbs, although other speeds will also be available.

There must also be a 'B' (for 'Bulb', or 'Brief ') setting to allow the shutter to be kept open. This can sometimes be done whilst hand holding the camera, but you will need the facility for attachment to a tripod as well. Because of this, ensure that there is a tripod bush underneath. To lock open the shutter a cable release has to be used (although some older cameras, and some of Russian origin, have locking devices on the shutter button itself). Check that there is a threaded hole in the shutter button to permit attachment of the release. These two features, tripod bush and cable release, are easily overlooked, and many modern compact cameras do not have the latter as standard.

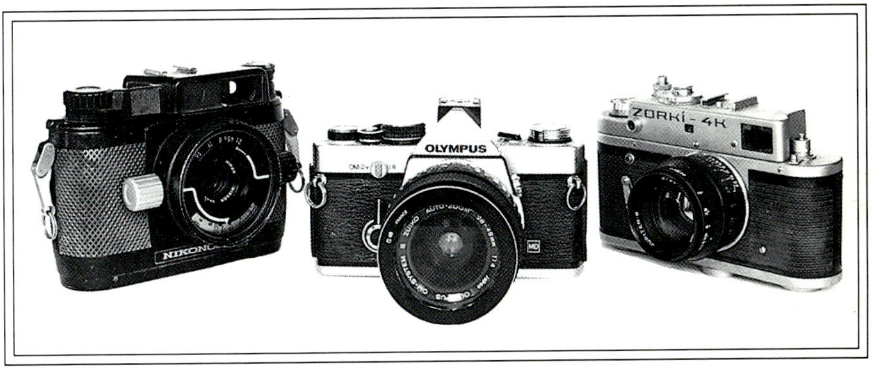

The Nikonos III is the best manual underwater camera, although expensive second hand. An Olympus OM2 is a light and compact SLR which withstands the rigours of caving well. Cheaper, rugged, but heavier is the Zorki 4K with its separate viewfinder. Each type has advantages and disadvantages to be considered.

Another detail that is often overlooked is the viewfinder. Some are very difficult to use in dim light. Check that it is as large as possible, and easy to see through. There is a vast difference between using the camera in bright and dim light; try looking at a dark corner of a room to make sure the finder is easy to locate and find the edges of the frame.

Obviously, you will be using flash for lighting, and this has to be triggered in some way. To synchronise flash to the shutter either a sync. cable (properly termed a 'pc' cable) or a hot shoe (which uses contacts in the base of the flashgun) is required. The pc socket is prone to become filled with mud, will tend to short out when wet, and the cables are prone to damage. The best choice is a hot shoe. Some older cameras have optional settings for flash synchronisation such as FP, M, and X. The former is unlikely to be needed. FP synchronisation was used with slow

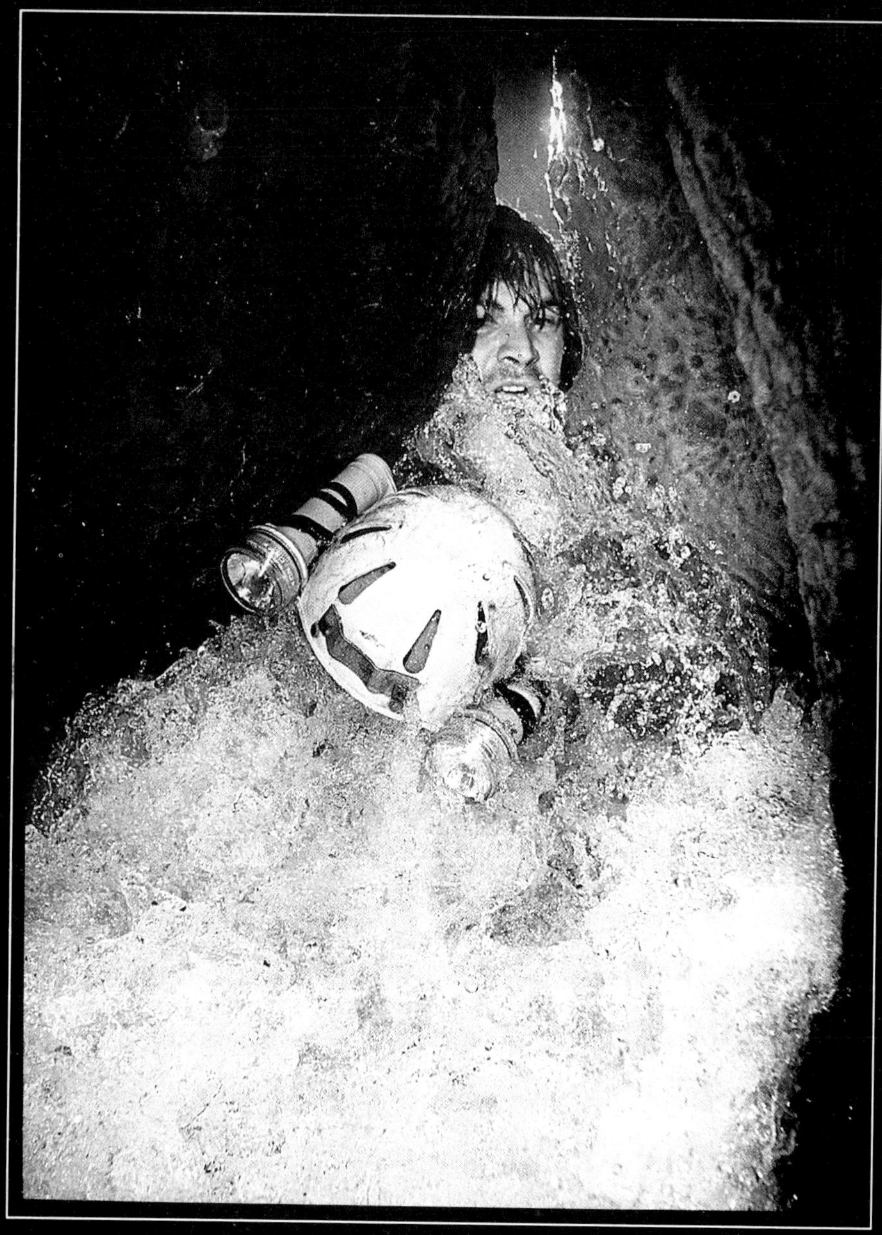

Bridge Cave. *A waterproof camera is recommended in situations such as these. A Nikonos III used on 'B' hand held within the waterfall, lit with B5, produced the silhouette. E1, E5 took the picture in the streamway. Notice the different effects of bulb and electronic flash on moving water.*

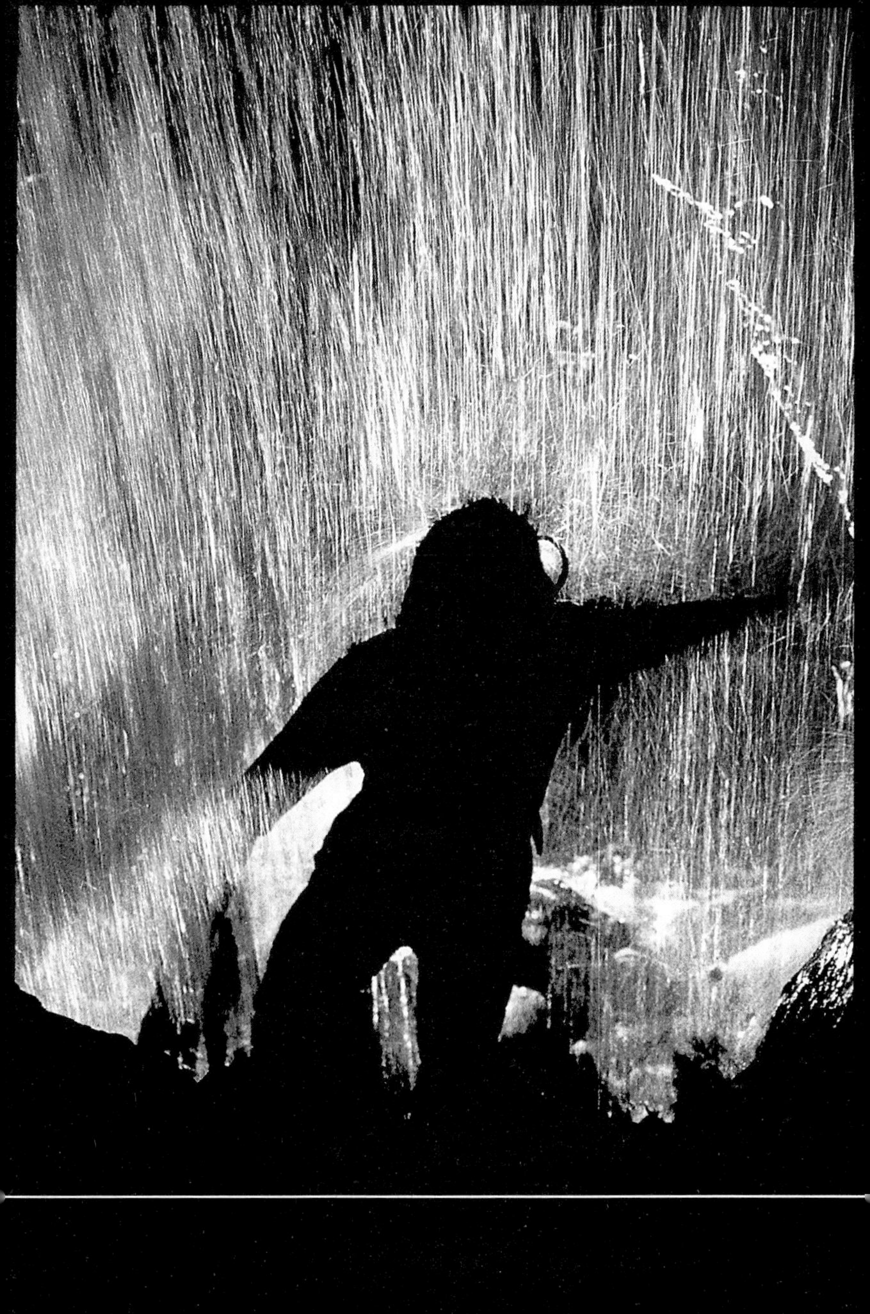

burning focal plane bulbs, whilst M was designed for use with bulb flash. When M was selected there was a delay between the bulb being fired and the shutter opening, thus not producing a blurred picture from ambient light reaching the film before the bulb reached peak intensity. X was intended for use with electronic flash. The shutter was opened, then immediately afterwards the flashgun was fired. For cave photography X sync. is ideal for both electronic and bulb flash, in the latter case permitting all the light that is produced to reach the film, and should be used in preference to M or FP.

With high humidity and a good chance of getting the camera wet at some time, manual cameras are to be preferred to electronically controlled ones. All electronic circuits are prone to failure in the cave environment, and a manual camera (which uses mechanical linkages) is a much safer choice when compared to one that has electronic contacts operating the lens aperture, for example. Light (exposure) meters can be useful for photographing entrances, but obviously are otherwise of little benefit. The presence of a lightmeter will not affect the performance of an otherwise mechanical camera even if it is broken or the battery taken out, which sometimes enables a very cheap purchase from a second hand dealer.

On the subject of electronics it should be noted that both the equipment and techniques being discussed are directed very firmly towards work in caves or disused metal mines, and certainly not coal mines. In the latter case dangers of explosion have led to any form of electronic apparatus (including camera batteries) being banned on safety grounds. Only specially constructed and tested flashguns that are 'intrinsically safe' may be used, something well beyond the scope of this guide.

Add to the factors required in an ideal camera the need for something as light, robust, waterproof and simple as possible, and the previously vast range has been cut right down to zero. It becomes a case of finding the best that you can afford with as many features as possible, not an easy task.

There are three main types of 35mm camera to consider; underwater, rangefinder or viewfinder 'compacts' (having ruled out automatic-only cameras), and Single Lens Reflexes.

Underwater Cameras

At first thought waterproof underwater cameras would seem to be the ideal choice. They are generally tough, and unlikely to suffer in even the dirtiest conditions. Aimed at the diving market, Nikon, Sea and Sea, Hanimex, Minolta, Fuji and Canon all include underwater cameras in their range, but even apart from the high prices drawbacks do exist. Many operate using electronics which will not enable anything but specialist flashguns to be fired, and these are expensive and generally huge. The Fujica HD-M and it's predecessors have no B setting. There is an integral flash, no further flash facility, and it is fully automatic. For general underground work it is not recommended, although if your chosen system and techniques use slave units (which are triggered by a camera flash and fire other flashguns without the use of cables) it becomes worthy of consideration.

The Nikonos range from Nikon is perhaps the best known of this breed. The latest model, the Nikonos V, has manual shutter speeds and 'B', but no shutter lock - you have to jam something into a gap beside the button, hold your finger on it, or use a strong elastic band to keep the shutter open. The shutter release can be altered so that it locks down by dismantling the button and cutting a slot in the edge, but this sort of modification on an expensive camera shouldn't be necessary. Advanced electronic circuitry also prevents the use of a bulb flashgun, which damages the printed circuit boards when the capacitor discharges. One useable camera is the Nikonos III, a smaller, rugged, manual-only model. Long out of production, second hand ones still appear, although they are expensive. If this particular camera, or an earlier one (the Calypso), becomes available then it deserves serious consideration. With these more basic versions bulbs are readily fired, and many of the problems of the later models are avoided.

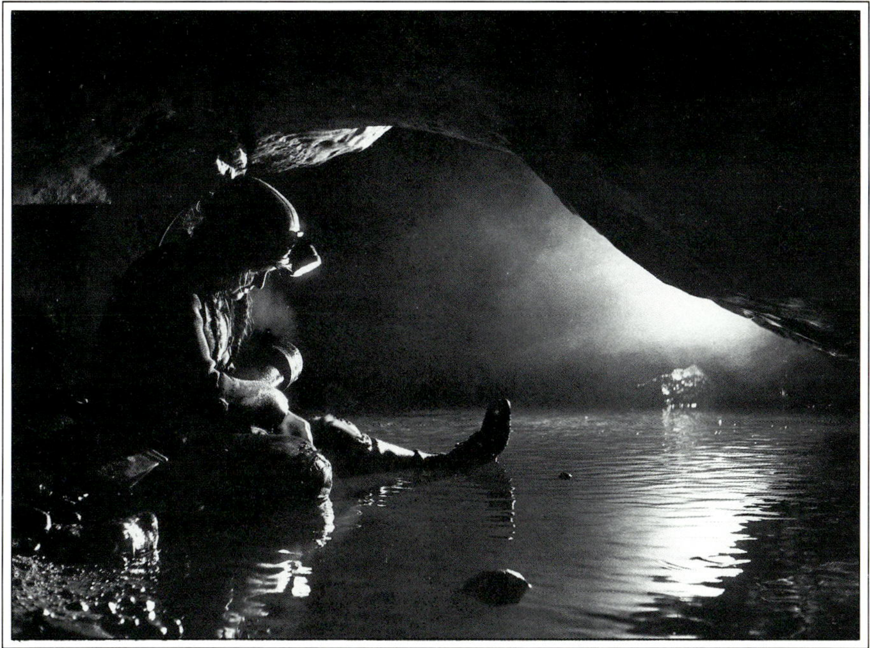

Ogof Y Ci. *Virtually any camera would be suitable for a shot like this, which was produced with a hand held camera on B and a manually fired bulb B4.*

Viewfinder Compact Cameras

Fortunately, the facility for total immersion is not essential,and with care most cavers will get many years of life from an ordinary 35mm 'compact' camera. This uses a viewfinder separated from the lens, and sometimes has a rangefinder to aid judgment of distance. A rangefinder is of little use underground. It operates using a double image which has to be matched up by the photographer, and in the dark this is virtually impossible for all but close up pictures. Additionally, a rangefinder can easily be knocked out of true and become inaccurate, and it is better to rely on judging distances by eye.

Advantages of these cameras lie with their size and weight, both being low. Disadvantages are the usually small and dim viewfinder, and an inability to change lenses. Many cameras are automatic (in which case ignore them), manual versions becoming increasingly hard to find.

Single Lens Reflex Cameras

The Single Lens Reflex (SLR), on the other hand, is easier to focus and permits different lenses to be used, although it is usually larger than those with a rangefinder and more expensive. It uses a mirror to view the scene through the lens, permitting accurate framing - especially of close ups - and usually has a large, bright, easy to use viewfinder.

One disadvantage often overlooked is the effect an SLR has when the picture is taken. As the shutter is released the mirror is raised, and the viewfinder blanks out. This makes little difference in daylight when the scene can be examined just before and after the exposure. However, in the dark of a cave environment this is not possible. When flash is used the photographer cannot see the effect he has produced (and sometimes cannot even tell if the flash has fired), as he would if using a viewfinder camera. Indeed, the ability to see the flashes being fired is very valuable, enabling fine control of any necessary re-positioning and evaluation of possible mistakes. If a flash is accidentally fired directly at the lens and ruins the shot, the mistake can be corrected on a second exposure if it is detected immediately. For this reason alone a rangefinder camera is valuable.

The Ideal Caving Camera

1. Full frame 35mm format.
2. Small and Light.
3. Rugged.
4. Hot shoe flash synchronisation or an X' setting is required.
5. Tripod bush and facility for attachment of cable release.
6. 'B' setting and manual control of shutter speeds, one being 1/30th second or slower.
7. Manual control of aperture.
8. Good quality lens.
9. Low cost.
10. Bright, easily useable viewfinder.

Consider;
A. Will an Instamatic with it's limitations suit your objectives?
B. Is the camera to be used above ground as well as under?
C. Do you need to produce medium format pictures on 120 film?
D. Do you need interchangeable lenses?
E. Do you need features such as dedicated flash systems for close ups?
F. Do you need an underwater camera for specialised use?
Answers of 'yes' to D or E will require an SLR.

When making your final choice don't only consider the camera itself, but also the use which you will put it to. If you want to take a lot of close ups, you will need the ability to change lenses and are limited to an SLR. If you wish to develop a small, lightweight system for fast use whilst on caving trips (rather than specialist photography trips) a viewfinder camera might be more suitable.

It is hard to recommend specific models, but of the viewfinder types Ricoh produce a compact with manual override controls, and the now defunct Rollei 35 range is a tried and tested popular choice. These were manual, very small and light, and had excellent lenses, though they were not particularly robust. Second hand, they are expensive. A reasonable beginner's camera which is both cheap and relatively easy to locate in second hand shops is the Ilford Sportsman. It is not as minute as the Rollei, but does possess most of the features that cave photography requires. As always, nothing is perfect, but it provides a reasonable compromise.

Suitable SLR's are more common. Zeniths and Practicas are large and heavy, but cheap and rugged. The Olympus OM1 is more expensive, but a superb manual camera granted first choice by many cave photographers. The various versions of the OM2 are equally popular, especially amongst those doing a lot of close up work since the flash dedication is excellent. If in doubt about what to choose, take a look at these models and compare others to them.

Lenses

Most underwater and rangefinder cameras have fixed lenses, usually slightly wide angle around 35mm to 40mm focal length, both of which are suitable. If you have bought an SLR camera, you will have to choose a lens to go on it. A 50mm lens probably came with the body as a standard, and it is far from useless, but a more popular lens is the 35mm wide angle. This permits the picture to be taken from a

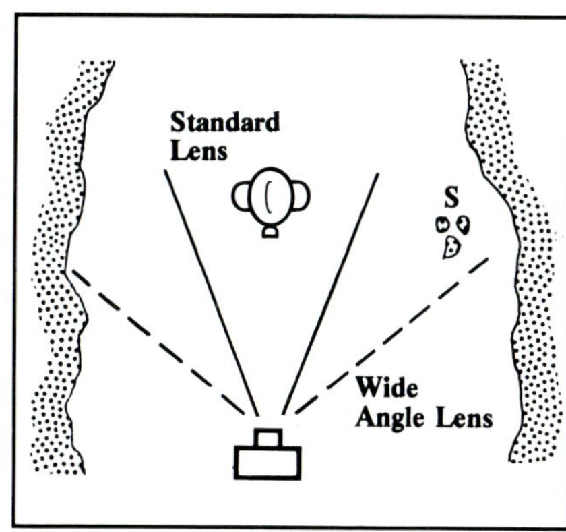

Focal Lengths of Lenses

A 'standard' lens for a 35mm camera is 50mm, which has a narrower angle of view than a wide angle lens, eg, 35mm or 28mm. The latter have certain advantages; they enable a caver to include more subject matter in confined spaces when movement backwards is impossible, eg, the inclusion of stalactites (S) which the standard lens cannot include. However, distortion occurs if too close to the subject. A good compromise is 35mm, and many cave photographers use this lens exclusively.

position closer to the subject, avoiding difficulties where there is no room to move backwards. Being closer, better use can sometimes be made of the available light output of your flashguns. Underwater cameras are usually fitted with a 35mm lens as standard.

Wider angles of lenses such as 28mm can create difficulties of distortion in some situations, and are perhaps better kept for specific occasions. There is an alternative to the 35mm, though, with the zoom lens. If it's range includes 35mm this is likely to be very useful, and permits exact framing when it is not possible to move the camera position, such as when looking down a shaft. Something in the range of 28mm to 50mm is best. Longer focal lengths are of little use since you would normally expect to be able to move nearer. If it is not possible to move closer then you will probably also have to fire the flashgun from near to the camera. With the loss of light over the distance involved, framing the picture with a telephoto lens is of little advantage since adequate lighting cannot be provided.

With light at a premium a lens with a wide aperture should be chosen. Lenses with a maximum aperture poorer than f4 (eg, f5.6) will create difficulties later on, although these are not likely to be found other than on old cameras or some cheaper zoom lenses. f2.8 and f1.8 are amongst the commonest apertures, and will prove perfectly adequate.

Flashguns

There are many similarities between cave and studio photography. In both cases the photographer controls the quality, power and direction of light, and the choice of the type of flash will dictate much of the final result.

The most widely available lighting in use is electronic flash, but flashbulbs still have many advantages. The choice of flashgun for firing a bulb is likely to be limited; cavers are forced to use whatever they can obtain. Electronic guns are more readily purchased, having almost totally superseded flashbulbs. Once again, there are some features to avoid and some which are useful.

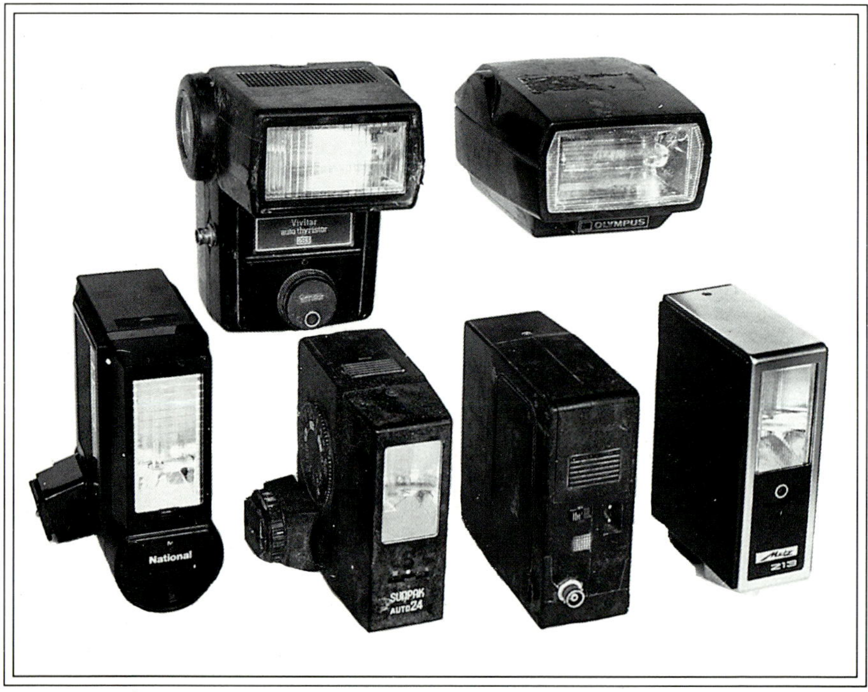

Many flashguns can be used for cave photography. A compact shape is important: The centre two guns are both Sunpak, the right hand one modified to remove the hot shoe and add a bnc connector.

The power of a flashgun is given in the form of a number; the higher the number, the more light it produces. This guide number is calculated by multiplying the distance from the flash to the object with the aperture required for a perfect exposure. This guide number remains constant for any distance or aperture combination. It is usual to work this out for a film speed of 100 ISO (ASA). When comparing flashguns, make sure that the guide number has been worked out for this speed, and also that the distance has been measured in metres. This is fairly standard, but some older guns had their guide numbers worked out using feet and consequently appear to have higher values. If the guide number at 100 ISO in metres is much below 30 it is likely to be too weak to be of much use.

In cave photography flashguns are not always physically linked to the camera, and may be fired manually whilst the shutter is open on 'B'. For synchronised flash the shutter is opened and the flash fires automatically, then the shutter closes. Check that the method of synchronisation on the flashgun is the same as for your camera, pc cable or hot shoe.

Most modern flashguns have a host of gadgets attached to them. There are bounce heads, flashing LED lights, large bulky handles - all of which are almost impossible to avoid buying, and are mostly totally useless for cave photography. One possible exception is the bounce head, intended for use when the flash is fixed to the camera. The flash tube can then be tilted to aim at a ceiling or wall to bounce light off it and give a more diffuse light source. In a cave this is obviously of limited use, especially since the flash is not always used on the camera.

Usually the bounce system takes up a lot of space and makes the whole gun cumbersome. However, the bounce head does have one use. If you use your flashguns with a slave unit left unattended on a boulder, the ability to rest the flash on it's back and then aim the flash tube wherever you choose is useful. Trying to prop up and aim an unstable gun which does not have this facility is both time consuming and haphazard.

There is little to choose between different electronic flashguns for durability, since all of them react badly to water. Choosing a compact flashgun with a regular shape will help when you try to seal it from the cave environment, and when you pack it for carriage.

Most modern electronic flashes have a 'computer' sensor built in. These 'automatic' flashguns are able to detect light being reflected back from the subject, and control further light output from the gun to give a correct exposure. Under caving conditions these sensor systems are of arguable use.

When relatively close to the subject, especially if there is a wall close behind it, light from the flash has an even surface to bounce off and therefore the sensor can accurately determine the exposure. A well lit picture is the result. Unfortunately, most of the time conditions are such that the sensor is fooled. The manufacturer, when the gun was designed, assumed that the flash would be used in an 'average' room with 'average' reflection of light. This hardly applies to a cave, and errors in computed exposure are frequent. A caver or formation in a chamber will be over exposed when both chamber and subject are pictured together since in this situation the sensor attempts to read reflected light from the background. Having a larger area than the subject, the sensor uses this to base the exposure upon, effectively ignoring the caver.

However, to have one automatic gun with a range of apertures on it's sensor control can be useful in certain situations. In any case, there is little choice in modern guns to enable a photographer to avoid the presence of a computer sensor. Thankfully, all of them will have a manual setting to enable full light output to be produced (or else simply blank off the sensor with tape to produce a manual flash). In case you are presented with the option of buying flashguns with or without an automatic facility, only one of your set need have a sensor system. For reasons which will be explained later, when two guns are in use at the same time they will have to be operated on manual. Some flashguns also have variable power settings, and can be fired at half or quarter power, and so on. This facility can be useful when balancing light output from two flashguns, or for close up pictures, but is a luxury rather than a necessity.

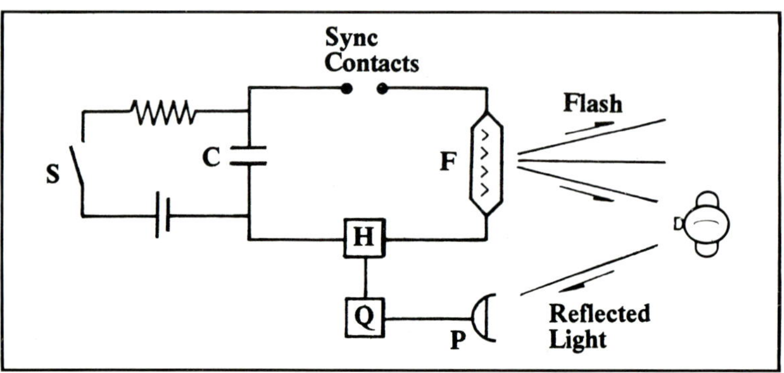

'Computer' Flashguns

Most modern electronic flashguns possess a 'computer' sensor. This is used to ensure a perfect exposure in normal situations. In this much simplified diagram, switch S turns on the charging circuit and the battery charges the capacitor C. When the sync. contacts are closed by a slave unit, test button, or camera shutter, the capacitor discharges through the flashtube F and a flash of light is produced. Light hitting the subject is reflected back to the photocell sensor P. When enough light has been received for the aperture and film in use this causes the quench tube Q to trigger a holding switch H that prevents the production of any more light.

Manual-only flashguns with reasonable power are no longer made in a portable form. For this facility older models such as those made by Metz or Rollei have to be sought out. These used integral rechargeable batteries, and had no facility for putting in replacements when they went flat. The whole gun simply had to be put back on charge by plugging it into the mains supply. Older guns which are not cared for correctly may not hold their charge for very long, and replacement batteries are expensive. For caving use, the difficulty is that if the battery is flat the gun is useless and just so much dead weight. Nevertheless, some cavers prefer these flashguns for their high power output, convenient square shape, and durability. In this area they are hard to beat.

Depending on the system you evolve, a small somewhat weaker flashgun can be a useful addition to your equipment. This will be used for fill in flash, or for firing slave units. Choose a cheap manual-only flashgun that is as compact as possible.

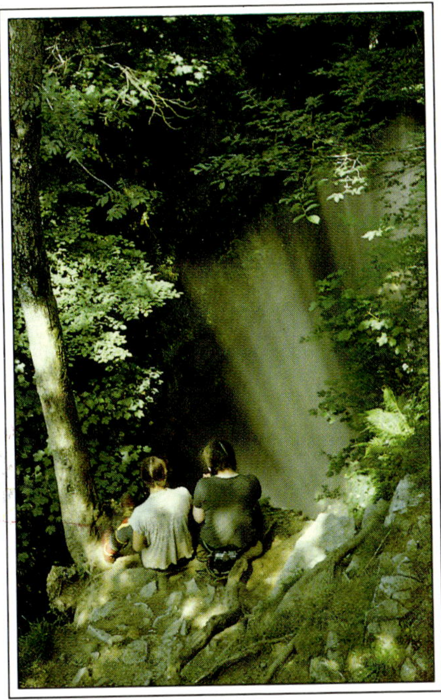

***Alum Pot.** A light meter is useful for photographing cave entrances, but is not required for underground work. This permits the use of less sophisticated cameras for cave photography.*

As a final factor to watch out for, try to obtain a gun which has a 'test' button, ie, one that fires the flash manually. Any flashgun which has both this feature, high power, and a compact shape, is likely to be useful underground.

Again, suggesting an ideal flashgun is difficult. Of the flashguns commonly available either new or second hand, the Vivitar 283 has been a popular choice over the past few years. Although not ideal, having a bounce head and being bulky, the power is reasonable and it lasts well. The shape of a flashgun is quite important. It has to be packed away when not in use, and if it is cumbersome the space wasted is annoying. Again, the 283 is not ideal, but nevertheless several cave photographers have used it with great success. Better shapes are found with guns like the Olympus QA310, the Sunpak 33, and National PE2850, the latter having a removable sensor as does the Vivitar. This can be an extremely useful feature, as it enables the gun to be held well away from the camera whilst retaining

Features of an Electronic Flashgun

1. High power.
2. Compact shape.
3. Durability.
4. Low cost.
5. Test button for open flash.
6. Hot shoe or sync cable to suit your camera.

Consider;
A. Do you need a computer sensor, or will a manual gun suffice?
B. Do you want a bounce head?
C. Is variable power required?

synchronisation. The sensor is left on the camera, measuring light coming back towards the lens instead of towards the flash, which may not give an accurate exposure if it is side lighting a formation. These features are all worth considering, but don't be put off if a flashgun you are offered is not one of the above models. The list is by no means exhaustive, and many other suitable flashguns are available.

The main alternative to electronic flash is the flashbulb. Bulbs are light, waterproof, and small for their power (which is likely to exceed even that of a large high power electronic flashgun), and they will prove invaluable. A combination of electronic and bulb flash is often the best way to light a scene.

Against these advantages, bulbs are bulky in the numbers likely to be used. Once common, they are now scarce and expensive. AG3's, PF1's, magicubes and flashbars are about all that are still available, but dozens of older sorts still turn up in junk shops. The best advice a caver could adopt when it comes to obtaining bulbs is that if it is capable of going 'flash', and is cheap, buy it and worry about finding a way of firing it later. Flashbulbs are still available in some photographic shops, or from chemists, but are very expensive from these sources.

It is recognised that not all cave photographers are prepared to go to the expense of using flashbulbs, and in future years they may not even have the option. Most of the suggestions for lighting angles and use of flash that are made later in this guide can be applied to a system which uses electronic guns alone, but whilst it is possible to do without bulbs it is difficult to over-stress their usefulness in permitting the production of different effects. Cavers should consider obtaining some for use when the occasion calls for it, even if expensive varieties are all that are available.

If you have a choice of bulb flashgun to buy, those that accept only a single type of bulb are less prone to go wrong than ' universal' types that will take both AG and PF fittings. If no flashgun is available there will be little problem in making something to fire the bulb, as will be seen later.

Batteries

To power the flashguns, batteries will be needed. Whilst adding to the cost, rechargeable nicads are worth buying early on since they quickly pay for themselves. Avoid using cheap carbon/zinc batteries since they have the power to produce only a few flashes, and soon begin to leak. In the cold it is not uncommon for batteries such as these to fail totally. Alkaline batteries are the only realistic alternative to nicads; they possess the necessary power, but are more costly than nicads in the long run.

Slave Units

A slave unit is a device that is attached to a flashgun either via its pc cable or hot shoe. It picks up a burst of light from another flashgun which is usually mounted on (or built into) the camera, and then triggers the flashgun it is attached to. There are no direct physical connections between the slave/flash and camera/flash combinations, for example a long cable. The use of such a cable is not recommended in the wet cave environment, for inevitably it will break or fail due to trailing in water and mud. Slaves are the only reasonable way of obtaining true synchronisation with flashguns off the camera.

Most commercial units fare rather poorly underground. They are made with the assumption that they will be used in situations where there is some ambient light, and are relatively insensitive so as to provide stability. If they were made more sensitive they would be continually triggered by the light of a household light bulb.

Some slaves work by triggering when a certain level of illumination is reached, a wasteful system in caves where light is at a premium. A better technique than using a threshold illumination in this way is to measure the speed of change of light. If the light intensity changes quickly, such as when a flash is fired, the slave detects this and fires the second flash. This latter type of slave can be made very sensitive to very slight changes in low levels of light intensity, whilst remaining electronically stable, and is therefore best for caving conditions.

One of the best types of commercially available slaves is that made by Sunpak, although others may be worth experimenting with. Some manufacturers have built a slave into a flashgun, such as Wotan's SC18, but either the power of these guns tends to be low (as with the SC18, which is nevertheless useful for fill-in flash), or they are very bulky. A good working slave system is invaluable, and if you intend

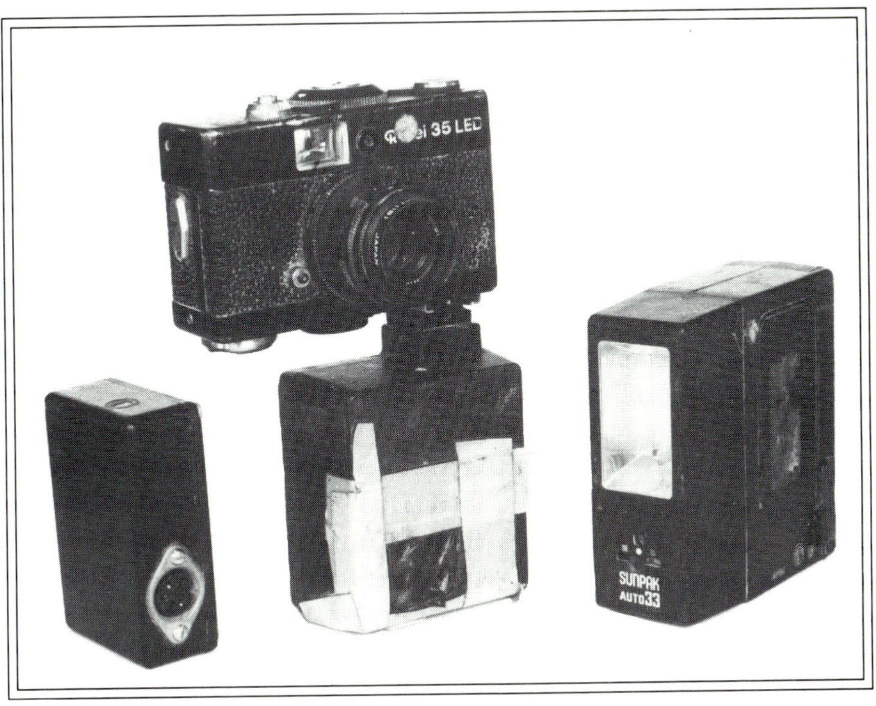

Cameras and flash need not take up much space. This set consists of a Rollei 35 camera with a small flash and infra red filter taped over the reflector. This will fire the Sunpak 33 when connected to the slave unit. Many of the pictures in this guide were taken with this apparatus.

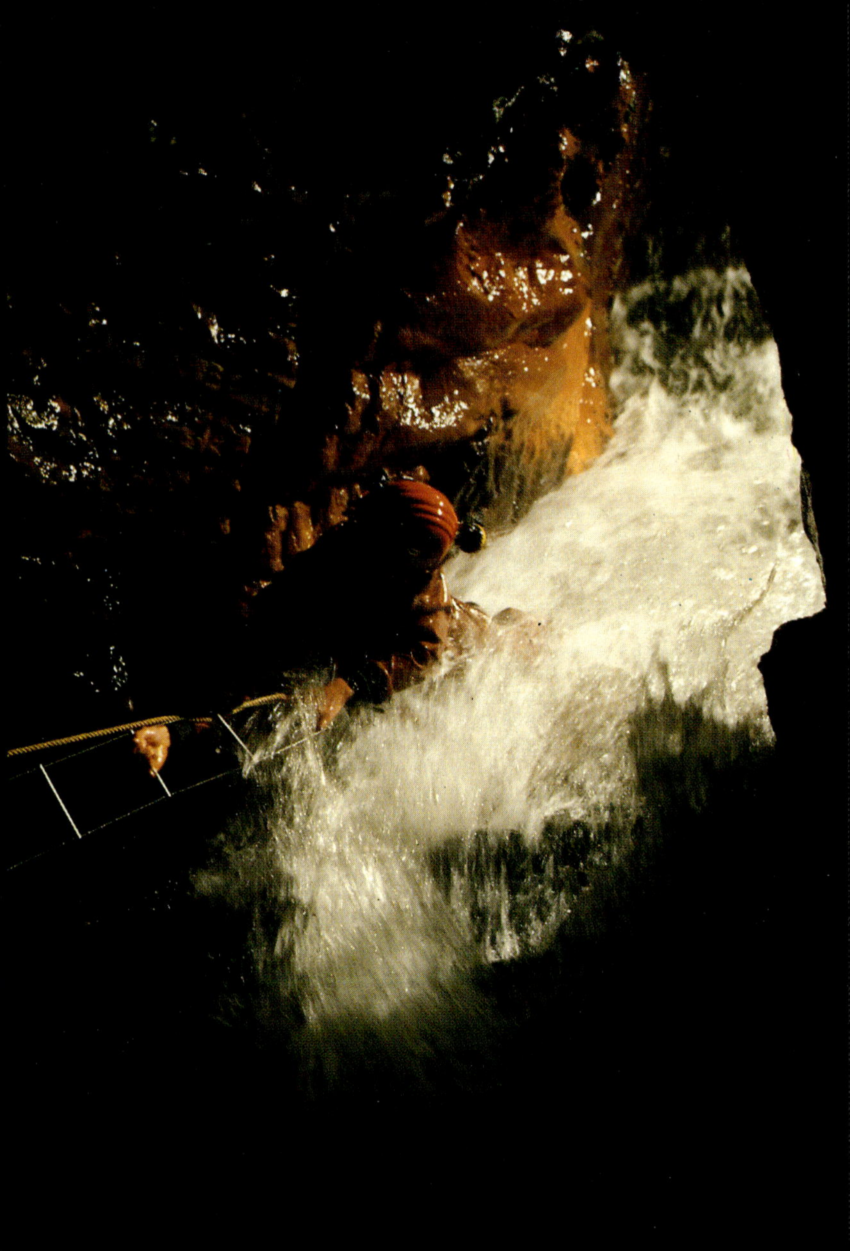

specialising in cave photography to any degree you should attempt to get one of the slave units specially designed and built for caving use by cavers.

Of the two types of slave in use, infra red and visible light, the former is more useful. Normal film will not detect the light from an infra red flash, and it is therefore possible to produce silhouettes and side-lit effects in synchronisation with the shutter without destroying the effect by using a visible light from the front. Infra red slaves will be fired just as easily by a visible flash as by an infra red one, since ordinary flashguns emit somewhere around 50% of their power in wasted infra red light in any case.

Obviously, the more sensitive the unit the better, but beware of those that are so sensitive they can be triggered by the slightest glimmer of light from a caplamp. This degree of sensitivity will prove to be a waste of time, lead to annoyance, and will detract from general usefulness. Good criteria are that the slave should trigger consistently at distances of at least 50 metres, and not be fired by stray light from helmet lights. The last is difficult to guarantee, since when a slave has the sensitivity required, fast movement of a cap lamp will sometimes fire it.

If the slave is being made up for you, or if you are designing your own, arrange to have a strong cable connecting it to the flash. This will enable the slave's sensor to be pointed in a different direction to the flash, for example when a caver must hold the flashgun against his chest but pick up light to fire it from behind. As such, this design is far more suitable than having the slave attached directly onto or integral with the flashgun.

Tripod

Although in many ways superseded by the slave unit, tripods still have many uses, not the least of which is their low cost compared to slave systems. They are invaluable for recording cave entrances, and enable multiple flash techniques to be used when insufficient slaves are available.

The choice of which tripod to use has always been difficult. Sturdier ones are large and heavy, smaller ones not being as convenient to use and unsteady when erected. Choose the largest one you reckon you - or your mate - will be able to physically carry and put up with. The alternative is to choose one small enough to get into an ammunition box. These will have limited uses, are frequently unsteady or too small to place the camera where required, but are often better than nothing.

The system of locking legs on tripods differs. Some use clamps, some spring loaded buttons, and some have a ring to turn which will tighten on the leg. In general, those that are spring loaded soon clog up and refuse to work, and do not lock at intermediate heights. The ones with rings can be difficult to operate with cold hands and sometimes slide if the leg is wet. Overall, the clamp seems to be the best system.

You should also check the spread of the tripod legs when it is erected. These should splay as much as possible. All too often a tripod has to be erected in limited space where the leg has to fit on boulders or an uneven floor. If legs can be locked at different angles this will help a great deal. Benbo make a tripod of this nature,

The Punchbowl. *Using an infra red slave to fire a bulb B4 retained synchronisation and the effect of flowing water.*

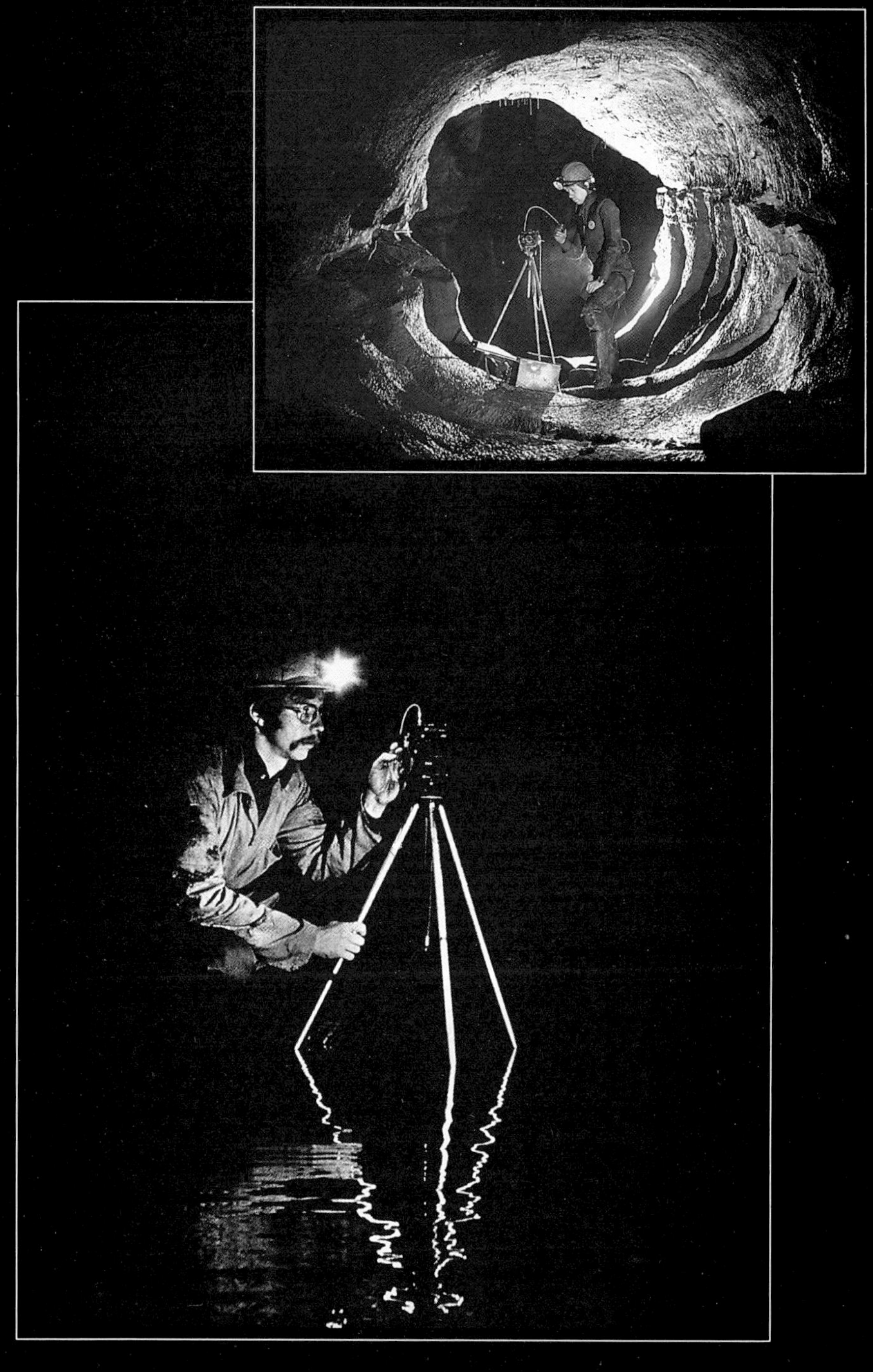

although it is expensive and heavy. Once again, which tripod you choose will depend on your own determination and techniques.

Cable Release

Despite their simplicity, cable releases differ greatly in their design. A button on the end pushes a flexible cable through a sleeve. The other end of the sleeve is screwed into the shutter button, which is fired by a pin attached to the cable itself when the cable release button is pressed.

When the cable release is pressed it has to be locked down to hold the shutter open on 'B'. Some releases use a small knurled screw to clamp onto the cable. This inevitably rusts or falls off with use, and obviously this type is to be avoided. The better designs use a spring loaded collar which automatically grips the plunger. The cable itself runs within a tube made of braided metal, cloth, or plastic. The latter is preferable since the others break far more readily. Lastly, check that the pin is long enough to fire the camera shutter and hold it open using the lock. For example, Rollei 35's need a very long pin to do so and 'ordinary' cable releases will not operate them.

Film

Initially, choice of film will depend on the use you put the pictures to. Firstly, decide whether you want to use black and white, colour negative or slide film. If you want prints to show around then colour negative may be the best choice. Black and white film can be easily used to produce prints suitable for publication in caving journals or books, and produce superb atmospheric pictures of caves. Slide film is used for projection in lectures but can also be used to make prints and be reproduced in magazines.

The choice of make of film to use will vary from person to person. All have differing characteristics. One caver will like the colours of Agfa, another Kodak. Colour, contrast, grain (the size of the 'dots' in the picture), and latitude (the ability to record detail in under and over exposed areas) all vary. Whatever your personal choice, the following factors are important.

Cave photographs tend to have a high contrast due to the use of flash, and this can be made objectionably high by using a high contrast film. It is therefore best to avoid such makes as Orwochrome or high contrast black and white films. Equally, a film of too low a contrast range may help retain detail in shadow areas but can appear unrealistic with respect to the subject.

Low contrast film tends to have a high speed, ie, it has a high ISO (ASA) and is very sensitive in low light conditions. The higher the ISO the more sensitive it is; the lower the ISO the less sensitive it will be and the more light is required to give a correct exposure. 'Fast' films may be found up to 1,000 ISO (eg, Kodak and Agfa), but detail suffers and results are comparatively poor under caving conditions. However, it may sometimes be useful to use the faster films, especially black and

*Using a tripod and cable release is an effective, low cost, method of beginning cave photography. In **Ogof Clogwyn** concealed lighting E2 was used. To light the tube in **Dan Yr Ogof,** E2 was hidden behind a boulder to retain a dark foreground. with B5 for backlight.*

white, if photographing large chambers when the lower requirement for light is more important than final quality. Very 'slow' films have higher contrast. Slide film in particular has inherently high contrast due to the presence of an emulsion which will retain it's saturated colour when light is projected through it, rather than being reflected from a paper surface in the case of a print.

The best compromise on film speed tends to be somewhere in the middle of the range, between 100 and 200 ISO for colour, extending to 400 ISO for black and white. For example, Ilford's FP4 or HP5 are good black and white films at 125 and 400 ISO respectively. Kodacolour Gold for colour prints, and Fuji's RD100 or Kodak's Ektachrome 200 for slides are all suitable choices. For high quality and detail use a slow film such as Kodachrome, at the expense of needing extra light to expose it. If you already take pictures you will probably have a favourite make based upon such factors as colour, sharpness, and cost. As long as it is a good one of reasonable speed, contrast and latitude there should be no problem in continuing with it underground.

In black and white there is a further area of choice with chromogenic films. After processing these use a dye instead of silver to form the image, and have to be developed in colour negative chemicals. Their advantage lies in their ability to record detail over a wide range of lighting, and can be rated at anything between 125 and 1600 ISO. Mistakes of exposure made by the photographer can to an extent be corrected at the printing stage, and the material has proved very useful when taking pictures of large caverns. In this type of photograph it is likely there will be areas of under and over exposure on the same negative, and these can be controlled when printed. Two films are currently available, XP1 and Vario XL from Ilford and Agfa respectively.

If you're a total beginner, try one of these films until you've learnt enough to experiment further and find something that is precisely what you want. Slide film is especially good to use whilst learning, since any mistakes you make will be immediately apparent. The film that is exposed in the camera is that which is viewed, with no intermediate printing steps. Faults in negatives, both colour and black and white, may be masked by printing, whilst other faults may even be introduced. Using slide film is perhaps harder than taking prints, for there is no possibility of correcting mistakes later, but it is more readily analysed by novices for mistakes.

In all probability you will already own some of the above equipment, which will help to keep costs down, but nevertheless give some consideration to assembling a realistic set of camera and flashguns rather than 'making do' for too long. As a minimum for serious work you will need a camera, and at least two flashguns - and preferably more! Accidents to photographic items inevitably happen underground and a spare gun can enable you to keep taking pictures and save a lot of time and effort in the form of a return visit on a later occasion. Add to this a tripod and cable release, or slave unit(s), and of course film, and the basic set is complete.

Dan yr Ogof. *A single bulb, B5, has a wide enough angle of illumination to light a large area of straws.*

Crag Cave. *B5, E7, fired by infra red slaves, combines the effects of side and back lights.*

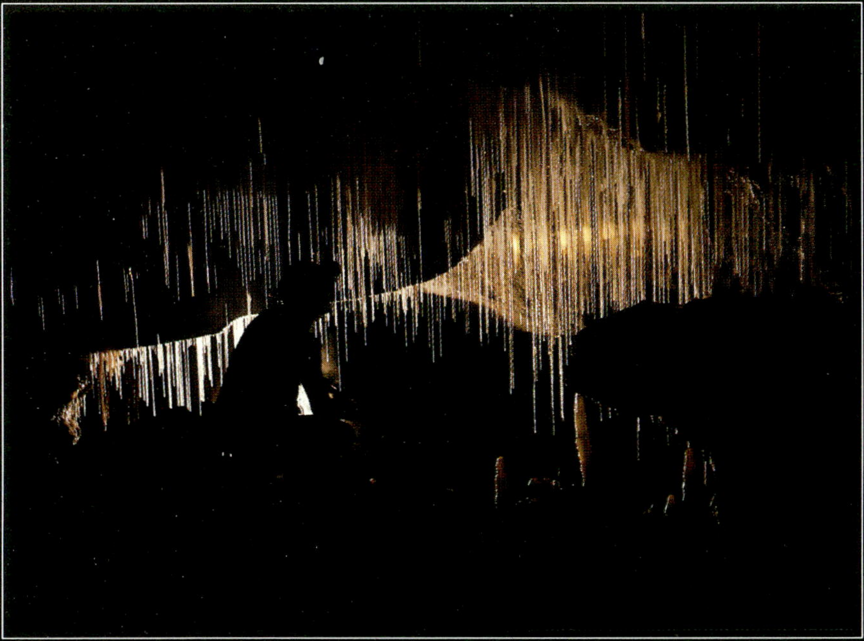

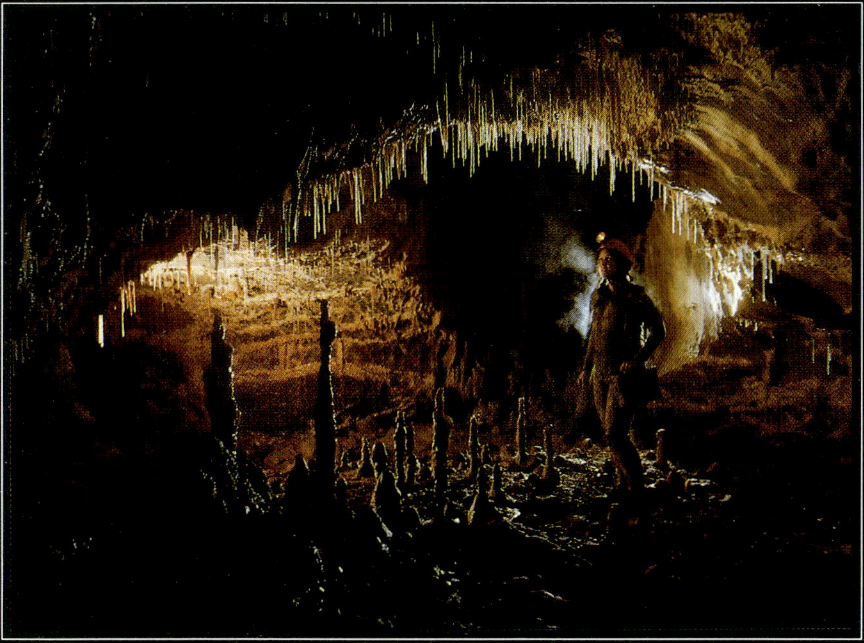

2
PREPARATIONS

Photographic equipment is delicate and needs protection both whilst in use and whilst being transported underground. Cameras and flashguns are expensive items, and prone to damage. Even if they inevitably become tatty, work and time spent in preparation before going into a cave will add to their reliability and useful life span. In addition, more reliable equipment will add to speed and efficiency underground, both of which make the photographic trip a great deal more pleasant for not only yourself but also for your fellow cavers.

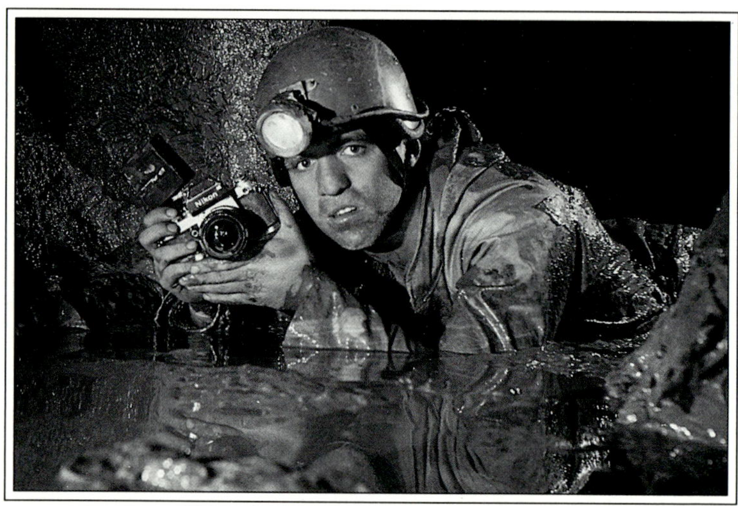

Ogof Ffynnon Ddu. *E8, B4. Cameras will be subjected to harsh treatment, and protection of some form is vital.*

Cameras

Cameras are prone to physical damage by being knocked whilst being transported as well as whilst in use, and perhaps the best protection for them is to construct a case made from wetsuit neoprene. Neoprene is light and waterproof, and will absorb moderate bangs. The shape of the case can model itself on the normal leather one made by the manufacturer. Arrange the case so that as much as possible can be left in place during use, since continually fitting and removing it whilst underground only increases the risk of damage.

Some cameras do not lend themselves to being contained within a case whilst still permitting access to the controls. For example, Rollei 35 cameras have the hot shoe and tripod bush close together on the underneath and are physically small.

A case that covered the camera would therefore interfere with their use. However, it would be an unusual model that could not benefit in some way by having parts of it covered and protected. The Rollei has a collapsing lens system which will inevitably pump mud and grit into the mechanism. It is far better to leave the lens permanently out and cover the lens barrel with a tube of neoprene. The whole camera itself could then be stored within a simple neoprene bag. Some cameras have a very large shutter button that could even be covered permanently and fired through the neoprene. Some variation of the above is likely to apply to your own camera, and is well worth carrying out.

Alternatives include using a housing or putting the camera into a bag of some sort. Underwater housings, unfortunately, are large and cumbersome, and very fragile. Controls tend to be difficult to use. In general, commercial waterproof housings will probably prove more trouble than they are worth, and should not be used.

Many general photographic books quote the idea of using a polythene bag to keep the camera clean. In practise the bag tends to get in the way, but might be useful for the odd occasion you wish to supplement your caving camera with a more expensive one, or if you know you are going to take your camera into a potentially destructive place. Use a large bag that won't hinder the operation of the controls, and if possible seal the opening around the lens using tape, a rubber band, or by gripping it with a screw-on filter. To help you see through, attach another hole in the back of the bag around the viewfinder either with tape or by pushing on a rubber eyecup.

The filter itself is the most important bit of protection. Either a skylight or UV filter will do. Being a piece of flat glass it is much easier to clean than the lens itself, and much cheaper to replace when it become damaged or scratched. It is poor economy not to fit one to your lens.

Electronic Flashguns

Protecting a flashgun is likely to entail a great deal more difficulty than a camera, largely because of sensitivity to water. The objective has to be prevention of the entry of water in the first place, but if the protection ever fails and the flashgun gets wet never switch it on. Extremely high voltages are involved and doing so could be dangerous to not only the gun, but also the photographer. If allowed to dry out when back home there is a good chance that a wet gun will work perfectly again, but not so if attempts have been made to use it whilst flooded.

Outer protection will depend on the exact shape of the flash. Physically, there could be a neoprene case made just as for the camera, but it is with the prevention of the entry of moisture that most effort should be made. Easy ways include sealing it within a polythene bag (self sealing bags are useful), taping all seams with pvc tape, or covering the whole flashgun with cling-film (which is highly effective).

However, the reliability and degree of protection can be raised still further if you are prepared to attempt some internal modifications. Take note, though. These will invalidate any guarantees there may be, and if you are not sure EXACTLY what you are doing these modifications are best left alone. Flash gun circuits are delicate and dangerous, and not to be trifled with. If you do so, it is ENTIRELY AT YOUR OWN RISK, and neither author or publisher can take any responsibility for any problems that may arise. It is up to the individual how many of the following suggestions, if any, are acted upon. Whilst the flashgun will benefit from the treatment, these procedures are not obligatory and a flash that has not been modified will still be useable.

Three factors may be involved in improving reliability under caving conditions. These are to remove any parts which protrude and are either wasting space or prone to damage or shorting out by water, the addition of better cable connectors to use with slave units, and improved sealing of the circuit boards.

Firstly, make sure the unit is fully discharged. With the gun switched off repeatedly fire the gun until it will not flash, then remove the batteries. Upon opening the case, find the large cylindrical capacitor and make sure you do not touch the contacts. Shorting these out may still release a great deal of power, and could even kill.

Varnish is usually used by the manufacturers to seal the circuit boards. This can be added to by coating all the components and wires with more varnish or paint, or even latex rubber from model-making shops. Silicone rubber, as used for bath sealant or repairing aquariums, is also good and can be peeled off if need be. DO NOT coat battery contacts, switch contacts, or the flash tube itself. The life of the gun in wet conditions should be considerably extended by adding this form of protection.

The pc cable which is often connected to a flashgun is very prone to damage, and if it is to be relied upon it is best replaced with a stronger wire. The best sort is a thin two core wire, or coaxial cable. If replacing it simply remove the old cable and solder on a new one, usually through a new larger hole in the same place. Sometimes it is useful to add a reliable socket for attachment of extra cables to the outside. If a suitable position on the case can be found, a miniature bnc connector (from Radio Spares, or its retail outlet Electromail) is about the best. This uses a bayonet plug, and is very reliable. To wire it up, transfer the wires from the hot shoe or pc cable, if these are no longer required. The shoe and cable can then be totally removed.

Care has to be taken with this operation, for sometimes switches are present in hot shoes and pc connectors. For example, on some flashguns the pc cable has to be shorted out by pushing it into its socket before the hot shoe is operational. In others, the hot shoe centre pin has to be depressed to complete the circuit. Check your own gun, and ensure you will be keeping the circuit intact before doing anything. Again, if in doubt it is best left alone, or else find someone who has knowledge of electronics to help you.

The advantage of removing any superfluous parts such as the hot shoe or pc cable is a reduction in the areas that water can reach and short out the circuits. Most flashgun failures seem to stem from water on one or other of these parts, something that their removal obviously prevents. Don't worry if you cannot or choose not to carry out these modifications. They're intended to add to the

Ogof Ffynnon Ddu. *Three flashes were used at E8, E6 and B4, all triggered by infra-red slaves. E8 was concealed behind a flake of rock within the picture.*

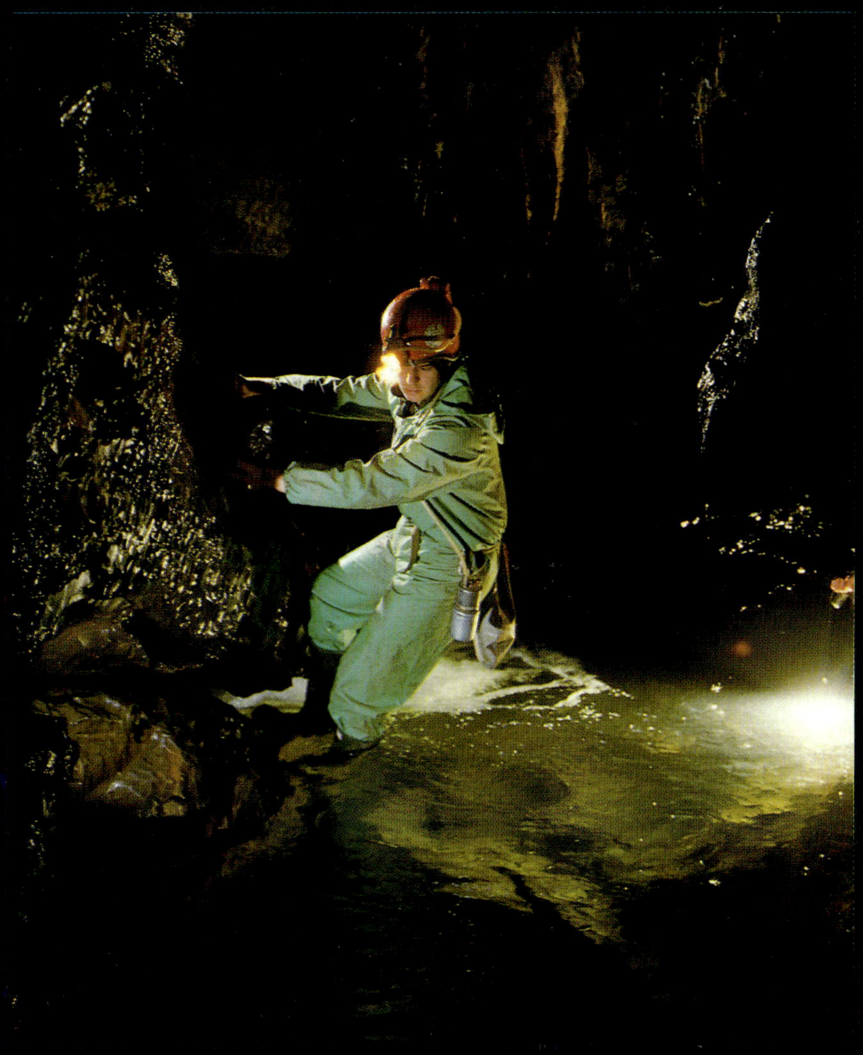

flashgun's reliability, and as such are not essential. Not using a modified gun does not prevent you from taking underground pictures, but means you will need to take more care near water. Nevertheless, always bear in mind the fact that electronic flashguns were never intended to be used in wet conditions and that without adequate care such uses can be dangerous both with or without modifications.

Bulb Flashguns

Obtaining bulb flashguns is becoming harder, and when found they are usually old and require a 22½v battery of some obscure type that is no longer manufactured. However, bulb guns are relatively easy to make and protect. Essentially, a battery charges a capacitor, which is used as a reservoir of power and helps to preserve the battery. A bulb has two wires or contacts that must have a current across them to fire the flash. The capacitor provides this power when a contact is shorted out. This is in the form of the test button, hot shoe, or pc contacts. The capacitor then discharges its stored electricity, which ignites an explosive zirconium paste within the bulb that in turn fires the aluminium in an oxygen atmosphere within the bulb itself. Only a few early bulbs used magnesium, despite popular belief.

In addition to firing with a capacitor, a flashbulb will fire when any reasonable charge is put through it such as from a 9v PP3 battery. Nicad batteries are preferable to other types since these are capable of producing high levels of electricity very quickly since they have a very low internal resistance. One of these connected across the bulb contacts fires it immediately. Some bulbs will not

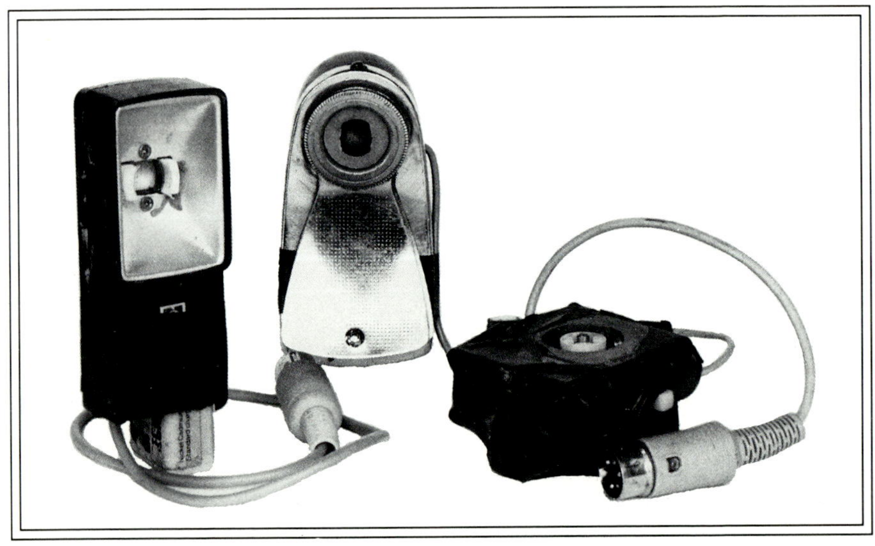

These bulb guns were made using a reflector and bulb holder wired in a series with a PP3 battery. A cable is used for connection to a slave unit.

consistently fire from a normal 9v battery, eg, some of the older PF1 types. Others can be fired by an Oldham cell, opening up further possibilities of self-contained flash systems.

Cave photographers often require flashguns to be manually fired well away from the camera. If the gun is to be used in this way it is possible to dispense with the capacitor and original battery holder and rewire the gun so that the contacts in the reflector go directly to a new battery and switch, all in series. It is relatively easy to rig a switch or button that can fire the bulb whenever wished, or of course via a

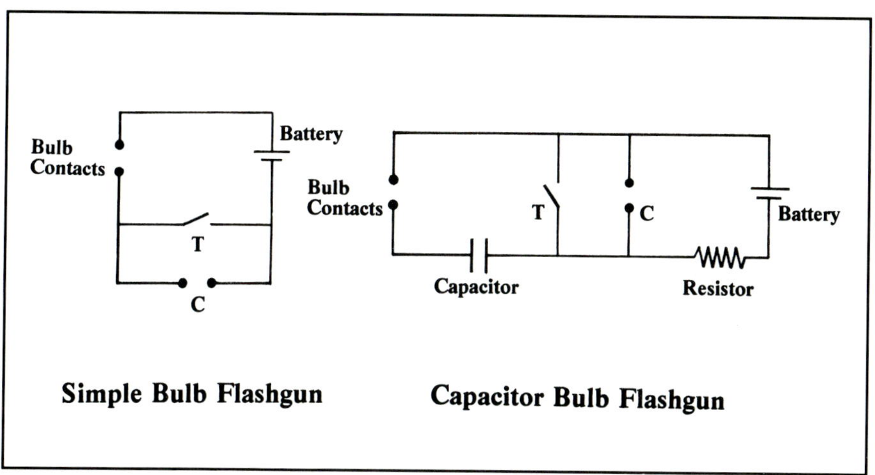

Bulb Flashgun Circuits

A simple bulb flash circuit uses a battery to fire a bulb by shorting it across its contacts. The flash is triggered by connecting contacts C, either by using a camera shutter or a slave unit, or pressing the test switch T. The latter is useful for firing the flash manually. A nicad 9v PP3 is a convenient size and voltage.

The addition of a capacitor helps protect the battery against shorting out and conserves its power. The resistor limits current flowing through the bulb so that it does not fire, during which time the capacitor charges. Closing contacts C or pressing switch T discharges the capacitor through the bulb. Charging the capacitor can only occur when a bulb is inserted. 18 volts or more are usually used in this type of circuit.

slave unit that has its own power supply. If the switch is operated the battery is shorted out and fires the bulb. The short is only momentary, since the bulb fires and breaks the circuit once more.

Indeed, a battery and switch can be connected via a length of wire to a bulb at a distance. If there isn't a reflector or bulb holder available, attaching crocodile clips to the contacts will suffice. AG3 bulbs are perhaps the easiest to use in this manner, since the contacts are easy to bend down and clip onto. Clips that are

Flashbulbs

Flashbulbs have been available in many types, sizes, and strengths. Most are no longer made, but may be found quite cheaply in sales or junk shops. The following list of commoner bulbs may be used to compare manufacturer's guide numbers (100 ISO, shutter speed 1/30th second or slower).

Bulb Type	**Guide Number (Ft)**	**Guide Number (M)**	**Bulb fitting**
Philips Magi/flashcube	*100*	*32*	*Cube*
Wotan XM1B	*120*	*39*	*PF Capless*
Atlas AG3B	*125*	*41*	*AG Capless*
Philips AG1	*130*	*39*	*AG Capless*
Mazda MF1	*140*	*46*	*PF Capless*
Sylvania AG3B	*145*	*44*	*AG Capless*
Philips PF1B	*160*	*48*	*PF Capless*
Hanimex AG3B	*170*	*50*	*AG Capless*
Philips PF5B	*210*	*69*	*PF Capless*
Wotan M3	*220*	*70*	*Pushfit Capless*
Philips PF5	*260*	*85*	*PF Capless*
Philips PF60	*440*	*145*	*Edison screw*
Philips PF100	*560*	*170*	*Edison screw*

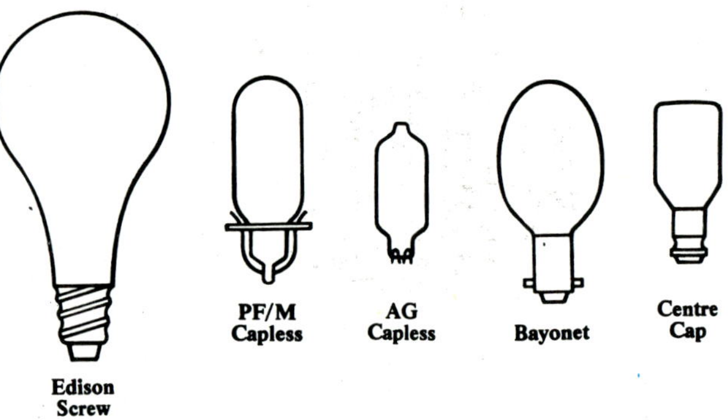

Note;
1. A 'B' suffix to the bulb denotes a blue coating of lacquer to balance it to colour film. Clear bulbs (no 'B' suffix) record a reddish colour on colour film if not corrected with a blue filter.
2. Bulbs contain a small blue spot as a safety warning. If this has turned pink it denotes a faulty bulb which may shatter on use.
3. Manufacturers assume the use of a reflector and some reflection from walls in an 'average' room. Some experimentation will be needed to accurately match the guide number to a cave environment. In reality this may vary greatly from what is sometimes an unrealistic manufacturer's guide number.
4. Flip flash and flash bars are essentially AG3B bulbs in a reflector, although power is slightly lower than an uncovered bulb. In this they are similar to cube flashes.

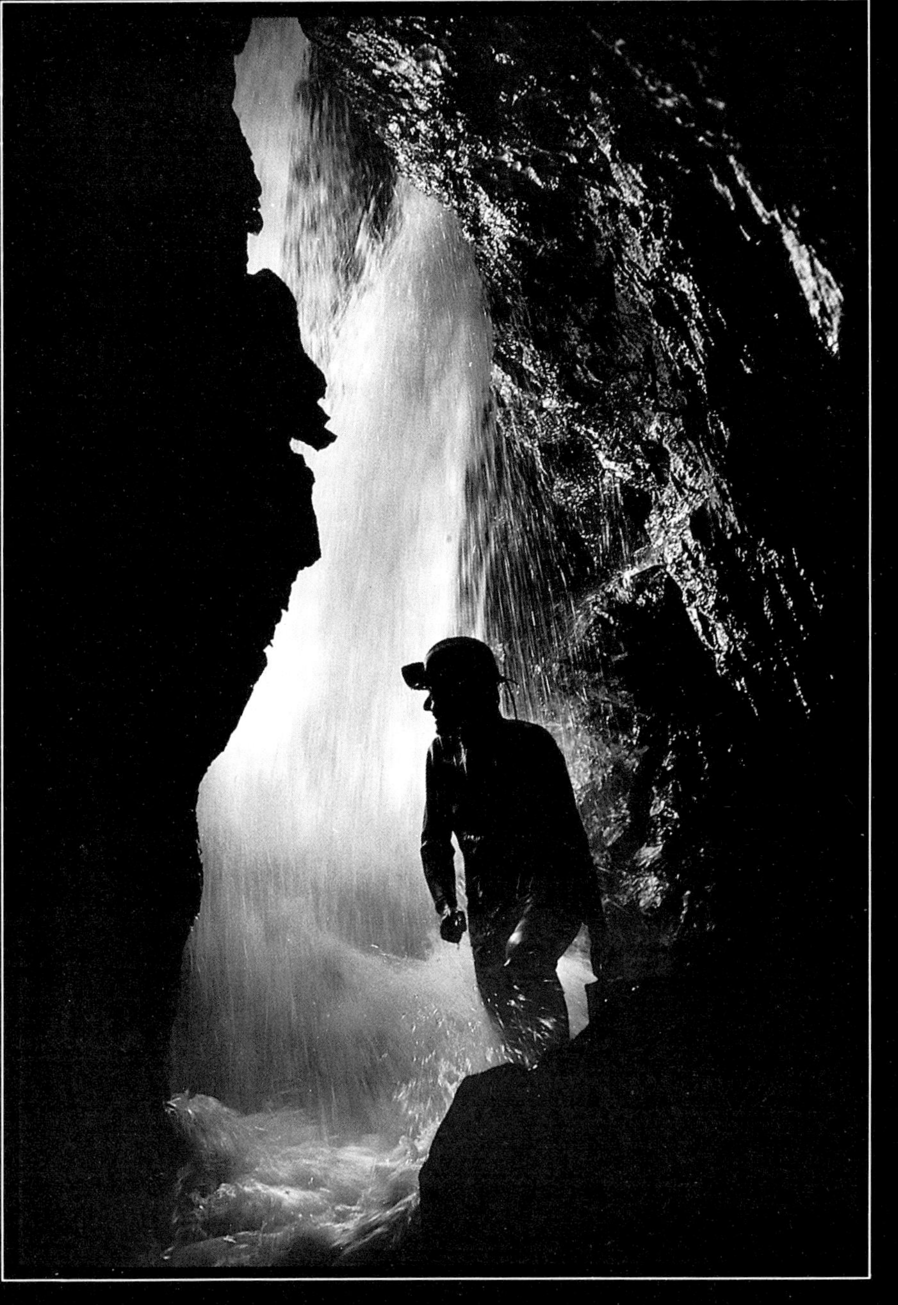

Bridge Cave. *A bulb flash. B6, fired through the waterfall has allowed the water to blur and give an impression of movement.*

rubber coated are the best to use since they will not short out on each other if they should touch. An alternative system is to use a capless bulb holder of the sort that is found on some car dashboards. These normally take push in bulbs, and are a perfect fit for AG3's. Some of the plastic used to clip the holder onto the dash may need trimming away so that the bulb is well exposed. A small lead weight attached will allow the bulb to be sunk underwater for special effects, where it will fire just as readily, being waterproof. A little thought is likely to produce many other methods of holding a bulb.

Reflectors can also be improvised using polished pieces of aluminium or tin, white plastic, or even aluminium cooking foil. The metal dish that pies are supplied in makes an excellent pre-formed reflector. Likewise, old torches can be cannibalised, or a carbide lamp reflector can be fitted. It is a simple matter to mount the reflector onto the clips so that the bulb is in the right place. If tin foil is used it can then be folded down to a convenient size for packing away. Uniformity of illumination can be a problem, but when using bulbs an efficient working system can soon be evolved.

Be wary of the battery power when using a simple circuit to fire bulbs. Since there is a momentary dead short in the system as the bulb fires, damage could be caused to electrical items such as slave units, if these are involved. A slow-blow fuse in the circuit may save damage of this sort. Occasionally, bulbs may internally short out and if left in the circuit the battery will be quickly flattened and damaged. This is one of the reasons for the use of a capacitor.

For a completely waterproof gun the whole unit can be set in resin or potting compound. If an ordinary battery will fire your bulbs (rather than a nicad) the whole unit can be thrown away when the battery becomes flat. This may be wasteful, but it is simple, will work, and the components that are lost cost only a few pence. Casting components in potting compound is a simple but effective way of sealing them, although rather final if access is later required. An alternative is to use silicone rubber bath sealer, which to an extent can be peeled off or cut away, thus enabling a nicad to be used which would be too costly to dispose of without recharging. One disadvantage with silicone is that it does not always set if the block is made too big - no air reaches the centre and the middle does not cure.

To fire an ordinary unmodified flashgun the pc plug can be shorted out if there is no test button. Whilst it is far better to cut it off and install a proper switch such as a 'press to make', a metal biro end or nail pushed in works well, although crudely. Attach one of these to the flashgun itself to avoid losing it.

Using the above designs any type of bulb can be fired. For example, flashbars can be triggered by attaching crocodile clips to the wires at their base and using a nicad battery. To gain extra power solder all the wires together to fire all ten bulbs at once. Ordinary bulbs sellotaped together will all fire at once due to the heat generated by the one connected to a flashgun. Magicubes, on the other hand, do not need a battery to fire them, and any piece of wire pushed into the base sets them off. With a little ingenuity there should be no problem with finding methods of firing bulbs even without the correct gun.

Finally, to save time and possible mistakes when underground the guide number, aperture and distance at which the flash (either electronic or bulb) is normally used should be clearly marked on each flashgun. These values will depend on the system of photography you develop. Details on calculating these are given in the next section.

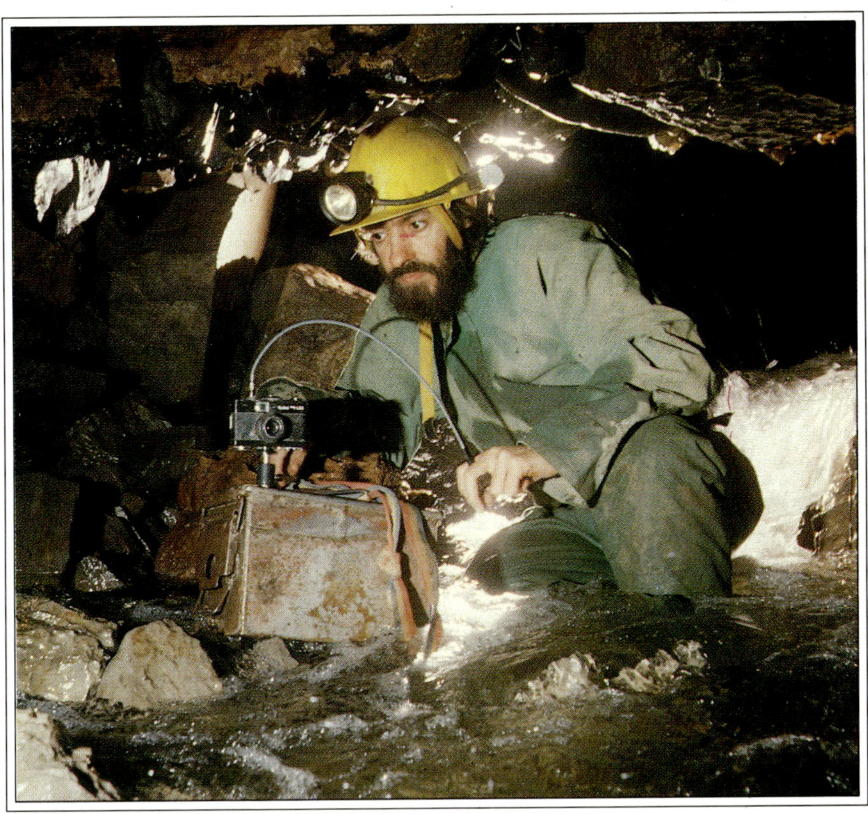

Bridge Cave. *Using a ball and socket head mounted on an ammunition box replaces the use of a tripod. E8, E5.*

Slave Units

The use of a reliable slave unit is a better idea than using manually operated switches, since in most situations it means that a tripod is no longer needed. Infra red units can be fired either by a normal electronic flashgun since this emits a high proportion of infra red light, or by a specially prepared infra red flash. In some situations advantages are gained by using a pure infra red flash to trigger the slave. For example, when taking silhouettes, no light is produced from the camera position which will register on the film.

IR light sources can be produced by taping an infra red filter over the flashgun. Unfortunately, true infra red filters are expensive. A cheaper alternative is to use red gel filters of a sort used in theatres, several layers of red polythene, or the black unexposed but processed leader from slide films.

As with flashguns and cameras, waterproof the slave unit as much as possible. The less water that can gain access the more reliable the unit.

Ammunition Box

Something is also needed into which all the photographic equipment can be packed for protection during transit. The most popular item currently in use is the ubiquitous ammunition box, which is cheap, made in three sizes, and is waterproof although rather heavy.

Alternatives are available, but these tend to be only of use in certain specific places. For example, in large open caves such as Mulu there is little point in carrying the extra weight of a steel container when a light plastic one carried in a

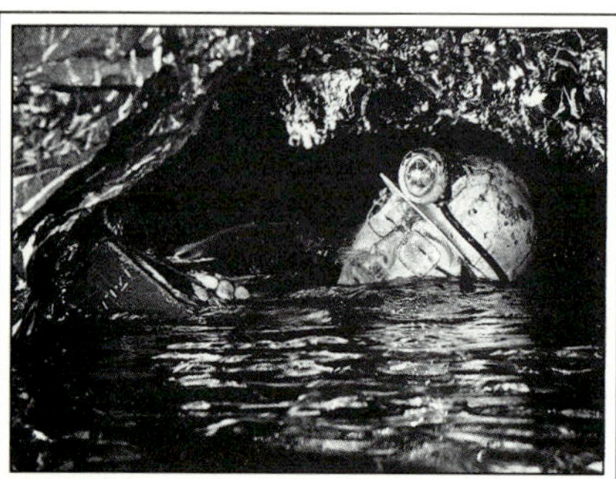

Ogof Rhyd Sych. *Careful preparations are needed both to protect cameras and set pictures up. With E1 only a poor picture resulted. To add the backlight in the confined duck a slave unit was floated on a raft and towed behind the caver. E1, B5.*

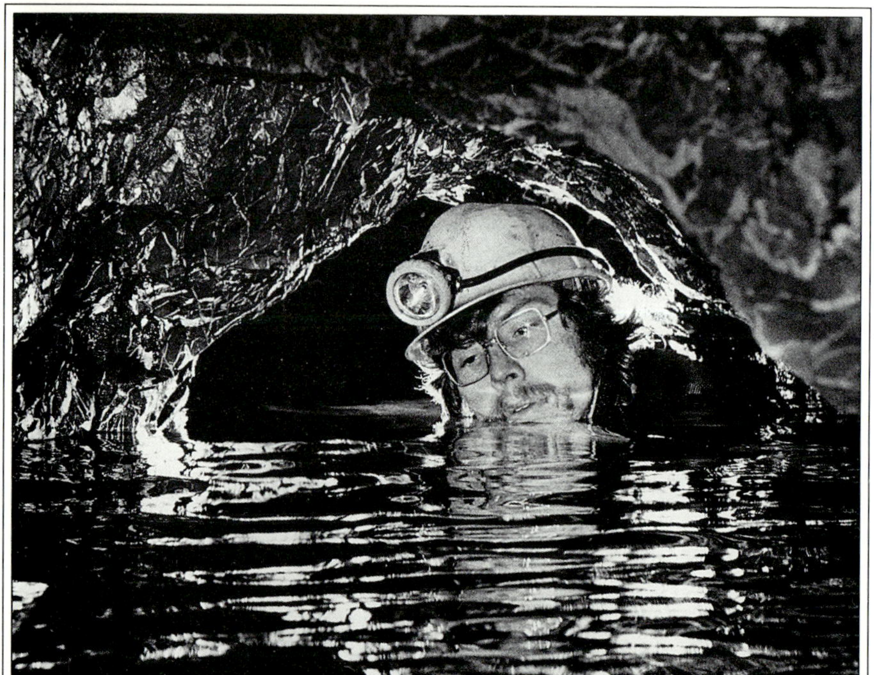

rucksack would suffice. Likewise, in a tight crawl a tube shape might prove better since it would roll. Diving shops sell a sealable watertight box that is supposed to be indestructible, and seems to take a good deal of battering. Tupperware boxes have been used by cavers, but the lids are not reliable under wet conditions. Plastic BDH containers, normally used to protect acid bottles in laboratories, can be obtained from most caving shops or chemical suppliers. These have screw lids, but again cannot be relied upon under all conditions. If you use one add some extra protection to the lid using an outer seal made from a ring of rubber cut from a car inner tube. Their use in any but dry conditions is not recommended.

If cameras are likely to be kept underground for any length of time it is worth considering sealing them into a bag within the container since even a well packed box may contain moisture. One technique is to use a length of inner tube, folded over once the flash or camera is inside, and held shut with a large clip. Silica gel to absorb moisture might also be used, but is rather unnecessary for short periods of time and is more suited to expedition uses, especially in the humidity of the tropics. Silica gel should be used with caution, since it can absorb so much moisture it will liquefy, and could then penetrate the very equipment it is supposed to protect.

Whatever your choice it will be necessary to line the inside of the container with something to pad the camera and flashguns and prevent them from banging the sides. Foam rubber can be used, but this has the disadvantage of soaking up a lot of water. Neoprene will work, or the cheapest method of all which is to use 'bubble' packing material. It is glued to the box and lid, and whilst it takes up very little space a couple of layers give excellent protection. Some cavers also like to paint their boxes so they show up easily in the mud, but this is of dubious value; the paint soon scrapes off, and the loss of an ammunition box due to being unable to see it in mud is unlikely.

Lastly, check the seal of the container by sinking it underwater. This should be done periodically; seals may perish or become compressed with use. Disasters with flooded camera boxes are not unknown!

Tripods

Little can be done to adapt or protect tripods, other than carrying them in something such as an ex-army rocket tube. However, it is usually possible to remove the ball and socket head and carry this in a box for extra protection, just the legs being carried outside. If slave units are used as a matter of course, a tripod is rather a redundant item. Sometime or other you will wish you had one, though, for time exposures of entrances, and so on.

One means of replacing it is to carry a small ball and socket head (at this size more useful than a pan and tilt head) which screws onto a bolt on the ammunition box. This might be inside or outside the lid. To fit standard tripod heads the bolt should be ¼" whitworth. The hole made to put the bolt through can be sealed with araldite or silicone sealer to keep the box watertight, and the thread protected on the outside with a wing nut. Alternatively, glue a bolt or screw from an old camera case onto the inside of the lid. It is difficult to use this system for exact viewpoints, but it can be invaluable for the occasional time when it is needed and does not take up much space or weight.

Packing

With all the modifications complete, the box can be packed. Avoid putting too much inside since it never wants to go back in the same way and will soon cause frustrations. Equipment always seems to expand in volume underground. Equally, do not leave empty spaces to allow equipment to rattle about. The top of the box is taken up with a towel. This is used to clean or dry hands before handling the camera, and dry the hands of helpers who are using flashguns. The best way of keeping the camera clean is to wear gloves when caving then remove them when taking pictures.

Don't forget to pack a few other odd items, such as spare batteries, a lens cloth for cleaning the lens, spare films (if you really feel like risking a change of film under muddy conditions), and a bag for used flashbulbs, which saves a lot of time trying to pack them back in neatly. Crushed in a strong bag they take up very little space.

Cleaning

Finally, it is always advisable to check out every item of equipment to make sure it works just before packing it for the trip. Periodically check the seal on the ammunition box for wear and leaks. Keep it greased with vaseline or silicone grease. Ensure batteries are fully charged, or replaced if need be. If you are using bulbs clean the contacts to ensure they fire first time. In particular, older ones may be coated with varnish to stop them corroding and this has to be scraped off.

Flashguns and cameras should have been thoroughly dried and cleaned after the last time they were used. Pay special attention to the sensor on electronic flashguns. If this becomes blocked the flash is liable to produce more light than expected when the sensor is in use. If anything gets particularly wet, for example by being dropped in water or being in a flooded box, open it up if possible and keep it in a warm place. Never operate a flashgun whilst still damp; it is dangerous, and could damage an otherwise salvageable gun. Electronic flashguns usually have small bits of foam rubber in them to hold the capacitor in place, and these take a long time to dry unless the gun is opened.

Get into the habit of trying to outguess problems before they occur, and finding ways of avoiding them. Anything that increases reliability will help to produce better pictures and retain your helpers for another day's photography.

Insurance

Even if you take the utmost care of your equipment there is always the risk of severe damage or loss whilst in transit or use (often by helpers) to be taken into account. Some insurance companies wouldn't contemplate insuring camera equipment for a sport such as caving, but many of the household 'all risk' policies permit the addition of cameras to the list and do not stipulate any situations they must not be used in. It is perhaps wise to take out a policy if it can be arranged, although it should be acknowledged that caves are risky places to take photographic apparatus and claims of a minor nature should be absorbed by the photographer. Too many small claims generally lead to massive increases in premiums.

3
SINGLE FLASH

During a caving trip there are likely to be various limitations imposed on the photographer, such as equipment that is both available and working correctly, pressure of time, other cavers willing to help, the nature of the cave terrain and consequent difficulties in placing lights, and the nature of the caving trip itself. If pictures are being taken during a sporting trip, for example, time will be very limited. Spending too long on a single picture that is unnecessarily complex or ambitious will only lead to failure and the annoyance of friends.

It is always important to remember that a cave photographer cannot work alone in more than a very limited number of situations, and that he therefore relies heavily upon his fellow cavers helping him to fire flashes and carry equipment. For this reason alone, avoid taking too many photographs during a trip which is essentially intended to be of a sporting nature. Reserve the more difficult multiple flash pictures for occasions where everyone realises the primary aim of the expedition is to take photographs, and keep sporting trips just that with only a minimum of equipment. Photography can then be planned accordingly.

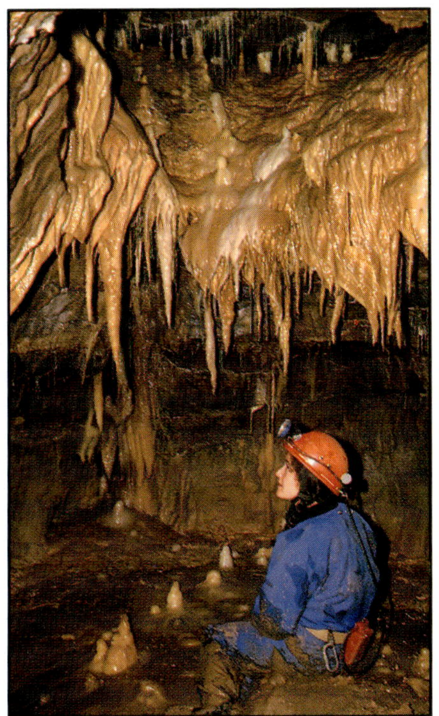

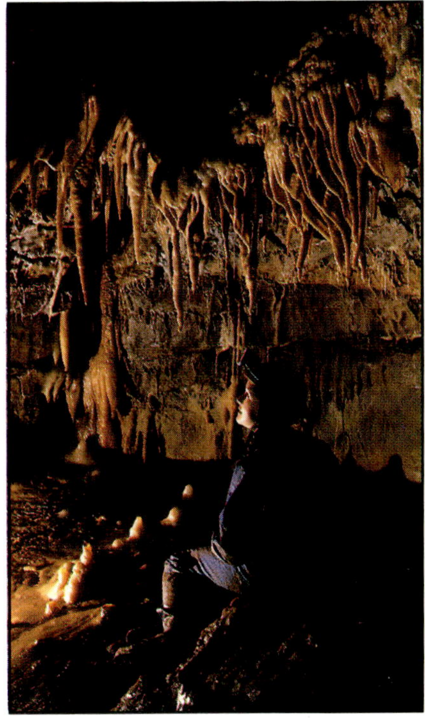

Ogof Ffynnon Ddu. *Moving the position of a single flash from E1 to E7 produces very different results. Choose the flash position to suit the effect you want.*

Using The 'B' Setting

Planning and organising a special cave photography trip does not imply that pictures will be taken using complex techniques. One of the most effective methods of producing a high quality picture is also perhaps the simplest, and involves a hand-held camera and single flash. It depends upon holding the camera shutter open on 'B' for open flash, during which time the flash is manually fired by another caver. If pictures are to be taken during a sporting trip, this technique is perhaps the most realistic one to use since with practice very little equipment is needed and there is no time lost in setting up a tripod.

To use the 'B' setting, the camera shutter has to be locked open. The length of time it stays open is immaterial, since in the total absence of light within a cave there is nothing to affect the film. When a flash is fired, the burst of light then exposes the film. The characteristics of the flash and it's duration control the final effect on the photograph.

Above ground the shutter speed dictates how sharp the picture is. For example, a shutter speed of 1/30th of a second will produce a blurred image of a moving object. A speed of 1/1,000th of a second gives a sharp image. In cave photography the shutter is effectively replaced by the duration of the flash itself. A slow flash of 1/30th of a second duration will permit blurring, whilst one of 1/10,000th of a second or faster freezes all motion. These speeds would be provided by flashbulbs and electronic flashes respectively.

In addition, whilst the shutter is open on 'B' any moving lights will leave streaks across the frame. For this reason caplamps are best turned off so that if a caver moves his head there will not be a white line in the picture as a result.

Working quickly, a caver can set up a picture and then with all the lights out hold the shutter open by hand. Keeping the camera trained in the right place can prove difficult without a reference point, so try to brace yourself against a rock wall, or rest the camera itself against a boulder or some convenient immovable

Producing Silhouettes

A caver holding and firing flash (A) will light the passage walls and cause some bounce-back of light from condensation in the air. This produces a silhouette of himself, and gives an impression of the passage shape. A bulb is needed in wider passages since an electronic flash is too directional and would not light the walls. A flash at (B) also gives a dramatic silhouette, and adds highlights to the walls without any midtones or colour, especially if the walls are wet and therefore more reflective. Firing (A) and (B) together combines both effects.

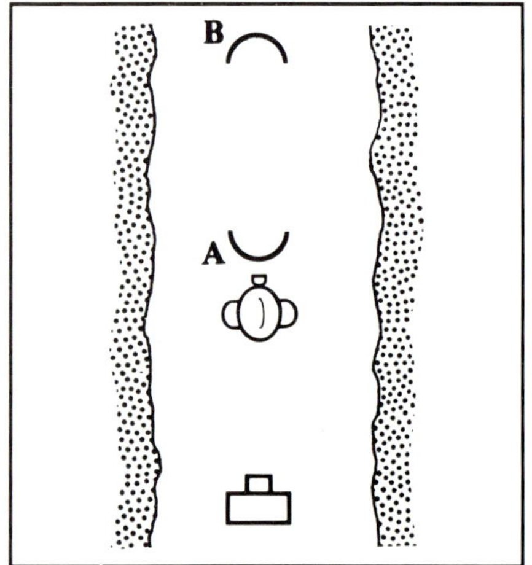

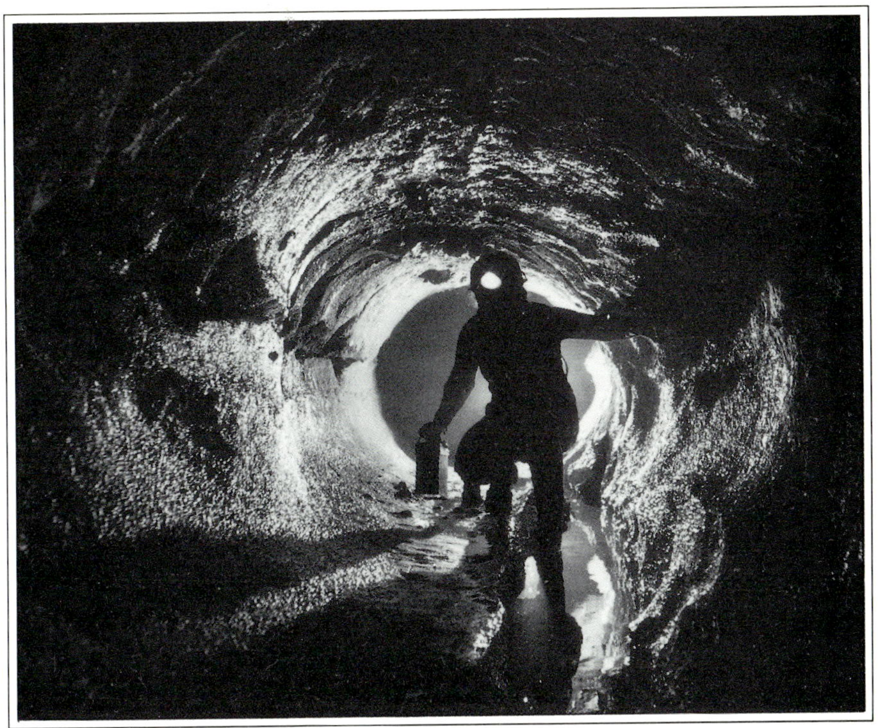

Dan yr Ogof. *B5 produces a silhouette. Using a chromogenic film, Agfa Vario XL, has helped avoid overexposure on the walls close to the flash.*

object. As soon as the shutter has been opened another caver with the flashgun fires it manually, then the shutter is closed once more. Crude this may be, but it is a very efficient, fast technique capable of yielding high quality photographs.

A good tip to remember is to always lean slightly forward for any of these hand-held camera pictures. Mist soon rises from wet suits or oversuits, and this will fog the air in front of the camera. Leaning slightly forward places the lens in front of the rising condensation, resulting in a clearer picture.

Using a hand held camera is not the only way of using 'B', of course. Similar pictures can be produced using a tripod, enabling caplamps to be left on if the people in the picture do not move. Using a tripod enables the photographer to double check everything and produce a carefully framed picture, and the risk of moving the camera before the flash is fired is eliminated. The cost of this advantage is in time, since the precise setting up of a tripod can be difficult.

Using 'B' has both advantages and disadvantages. In both cases, hand-held or tripod-mounted camera, the tendency is to produce a picture with a static pose since there is little leeway for movement of the subject. This may not be too important if the lighting has been handled imaginatively, and would not apply to photographs of formations. There is still the risk of a caver moving and recording a streak of light from his caplamp on the film. Obviously, this could be avoided if the lamp is

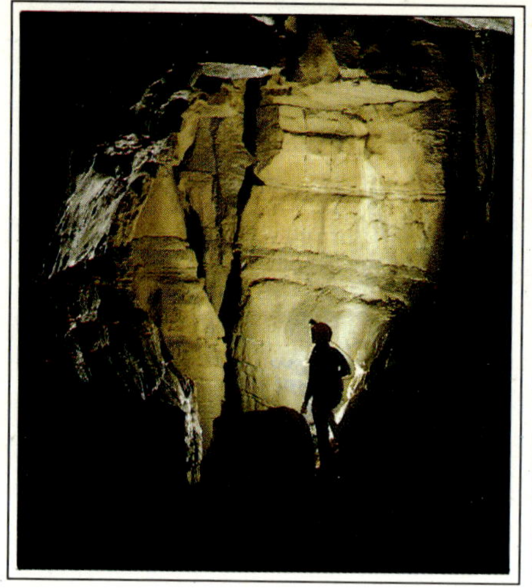

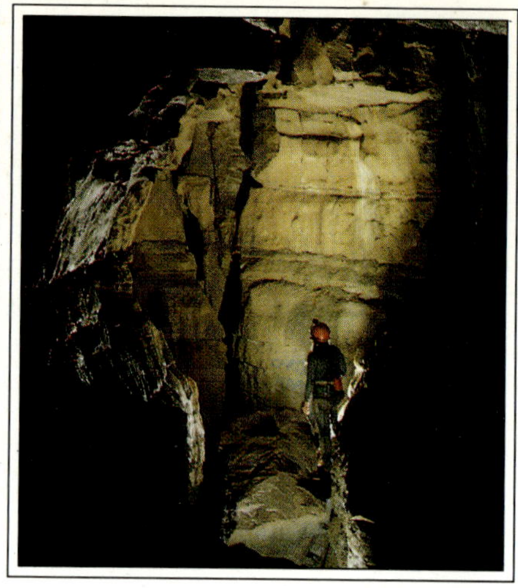

Chartist Cave. *The caver firing E1, with B5 aimed back towards the camera, produce a silhouette together. The addition of a third flash below the camera adds foreground detail. Individual flashes can be used to build up pictures in this way.*

switched off before taking a picture. The result may not be what is desired. Nothing looks more unnatural than a caving picture with a caver striding down a streamway with no light on. The alternative is either an even more static pose to avoid movement of a caplamp, or the risk of a ruined picture. If it can be arranged, though, as long as the shutter is not open for too long a pleasant glow of light from a caplamp enhances any picture.

Advantages of Slave Units

Both speed and freedom to position lights and models are conferred by the use of a slave unit. This does mean the use of a second flash on the camera to trigger the slave, but if this is infra red there will be no visible light produced to affect the film. The flash is synchronised to the shutter, so 'B' is no longer used. The effect is similar to the use of 'B' with a single manually operated flashgun, but there are advantages to using slaves which eliminate many of the disadvantages of using 'B'.

For example, the model can both keep his caplamp turned on and move about without leaving streaks of light on the film. With lights left on the photographer can readily see what he is taking a picture of, or at worst have a reference point to keep the hand-held camera correctly aimed. There is the possibility of producing action photographs with greater ease, and natural poses can be produced by allowing a caver to walk forwards and taking the picture when it looks right.

In confined spaces techniques are limited. At ***Gough's Cave*** *the background was close to the subject and allowed the use of a 'computer' flash. E1, B5 was used at both* ***Ogof Pasg*** *and* ***Ogof Cynnes.*** *Conditions like these require a well protected camera.*

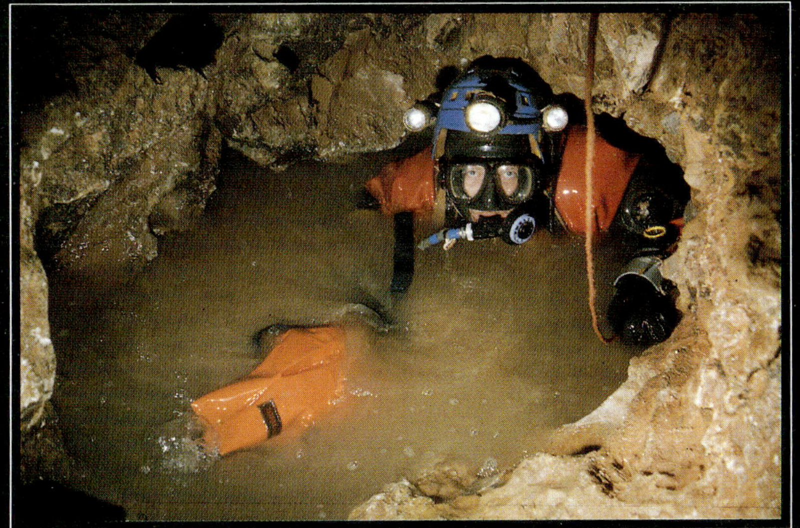

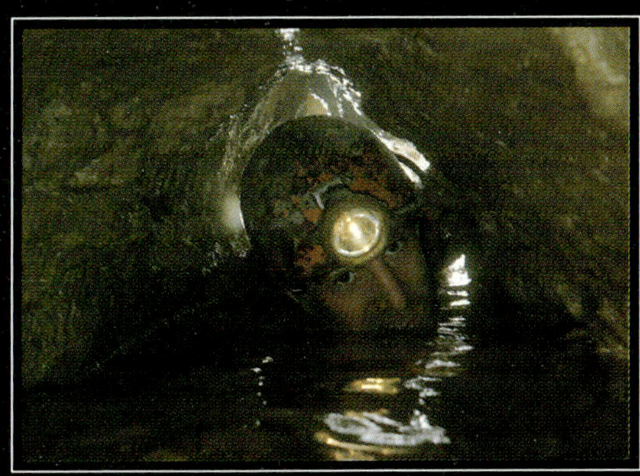

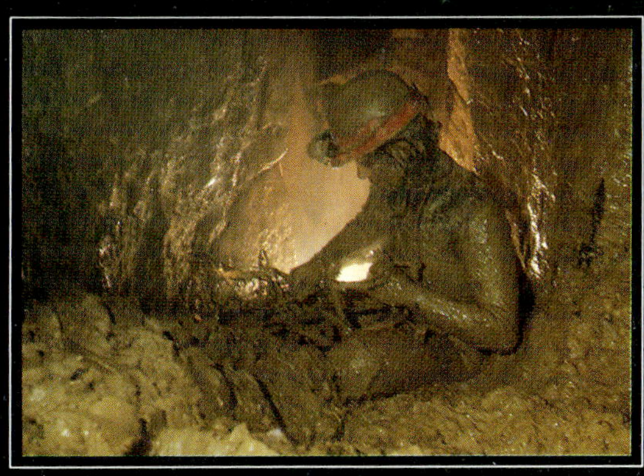

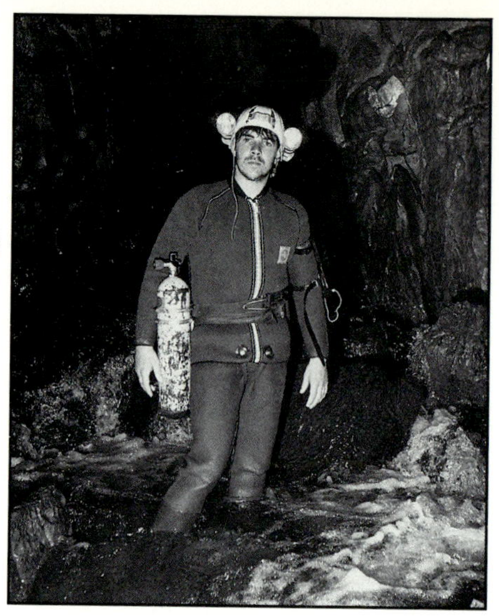

Bridge Cave. *A single flash, E1, produces a low contrast picture. E3 and E5 produce better lighting effects with higher contrast and relief.*

Cavers on ladders, ropes, or climbs can be photographed in action in situations where it would be difficult for them to maintain the static pose often required by the use of a tripod. Indeed, pictures can be taken in situations where it would be impossible to erect a tripod at all.

Placing Lights

Whatever the technique adopted, 'B' either hand held or on tripod, or using a slave unit, it is the light placement that is crucial. The whole effect of the final picture will depend on this, and whilst the following is not intended to be an inviolate set of rules it does include advice which will lead to the production of a good basic picture. Learn the ground rules first, then experiment for yourself.

Above all else there is one basic rule when it comes to flashgun placement; keep the light well away from the camera. Cave air is humid and may well have further moisture in it from condensing breath. Each droplet of moisture will reflect light back towards its source. If this is near the camera the result is a flat, low contrast, uninspiring whitish mist that occludes the subject. Driving a car in fog with headlights on full beam gives the same basic impression.

Additionally, if the caver in the picture is looking towards the camera, light will be reflected from the blood-rich retina at the back of the eye, producing a ghastly effect called 'red eye'. This results in a person with bright red staring eyes on the photograph. In both cases, red eye and contrast problems, moving the flash away from the camera eliminates the effect.

The flash need not be much to one side of the camera to accomplish this. It can be fired in almost a direct line with the camera and subject, as long as it is not too close (ie, from within the picture by another caver). A caver that fires a flash aimed away from (but in line with) the camera from within the picture area leaves himself

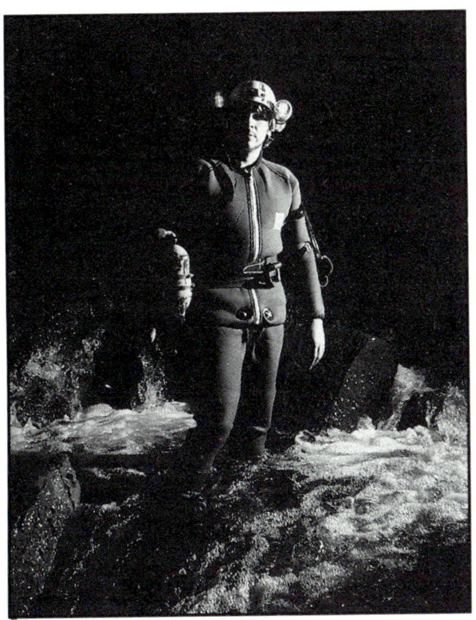

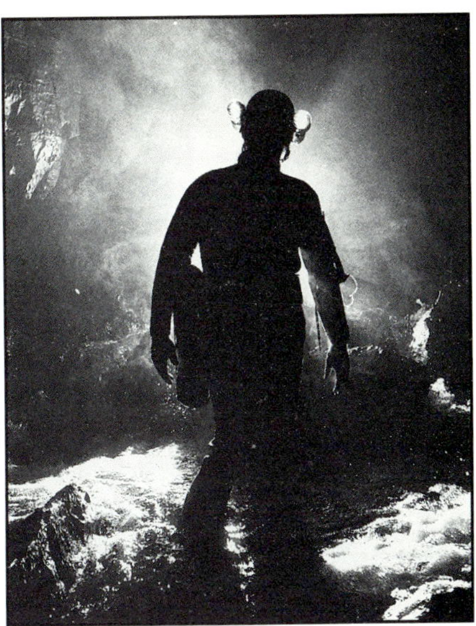

as a silhouette. The resulting photograph is produced with dark edges that helps it's composition. To ensure the avoidance of red eye in this case, anyone that is lit by the flash should make sure they are not looking directly towards the camera.

The further away to the side the flash is taken, the more pronounced the effect of added relief and side lighting in the picture, until the flashgun is eventually placed directly behind the subject. This gives pure backlighting, useful for producing rim-lit effects, showing up condensation in the air, and silhouettes. Highlights are added to rock walls and roofs, spray glistens pure white. Indeed, the effect works best when the air is filled with condensation and light can be scattered.

It is this light that shows up mist rising from damp wet suits and the condensing warm air from a caver's breath. The effect is using, and depending upon, the very factors that prevented the placement of the flash on the camera in the first place. As such, the addition of this light grants a special feature that distinguishes a cave photograph from pictures taken in the dark in more mundane locations.

Both side and back lighting add to the drama of a photograph, but it is not only the actual placing of the lights that is important. The quality of the actual light being produced should also be considered.

Flashbulbs or Electronic Flash?

There are vast differences between light from a bulb and an electronic flash. Three factors are involved: power or intensity, angle of illumination, and duration of the flash. Generally speaking, bulbs have greater power than an electronic unit. That is, they emit more light during the flash, but the amount reaching the subject depends not only on the type of bulb but on the reflector used. Without a reflector, light is given out over 360°, half of it going in the wrong direction. With a reflector, the beam of light can be directed where desired. Just keeping the reflector

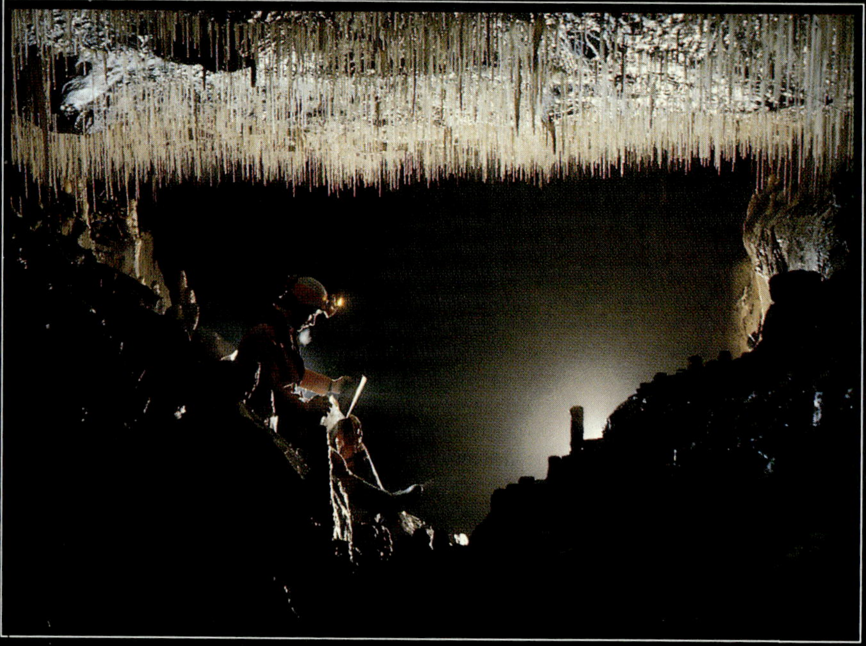

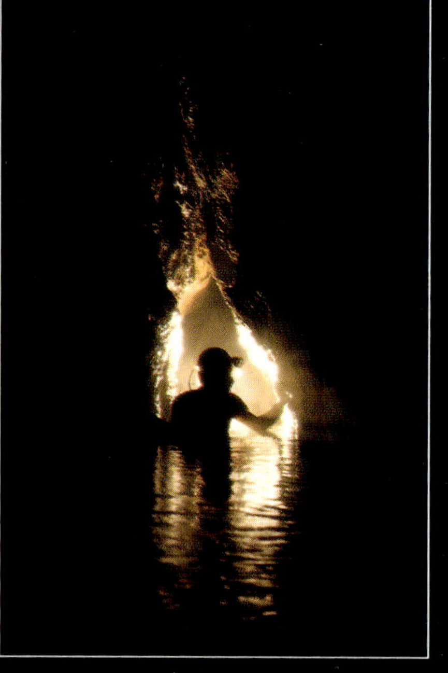

Easgill Caverns. *E5 has backlit the caver, B4 lights the roof.*

Bridge Cave. *B5 and E8 combine their effects to give a sharp foreground, but blurred water. The electronic flash was used in 'computer' mode, the light from the bulb not being fast enough to interfere and cause an incorrect exposure.*

Llygad Llwchwr*. A single flash, B5, is enough to silhouette the caver and show the ripples on the water.*

Ogof Ffynnon Ddu. *B5, E4 has produced enough detail in the rock and caver without destroying the atmosphere of a backlit picture.*

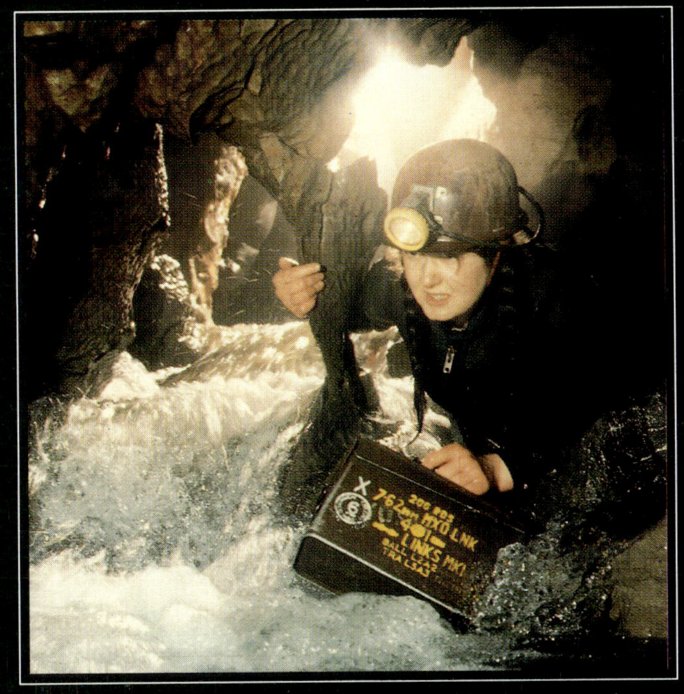
200 RDS
7.62mm MXD LNK
LINKS MK1

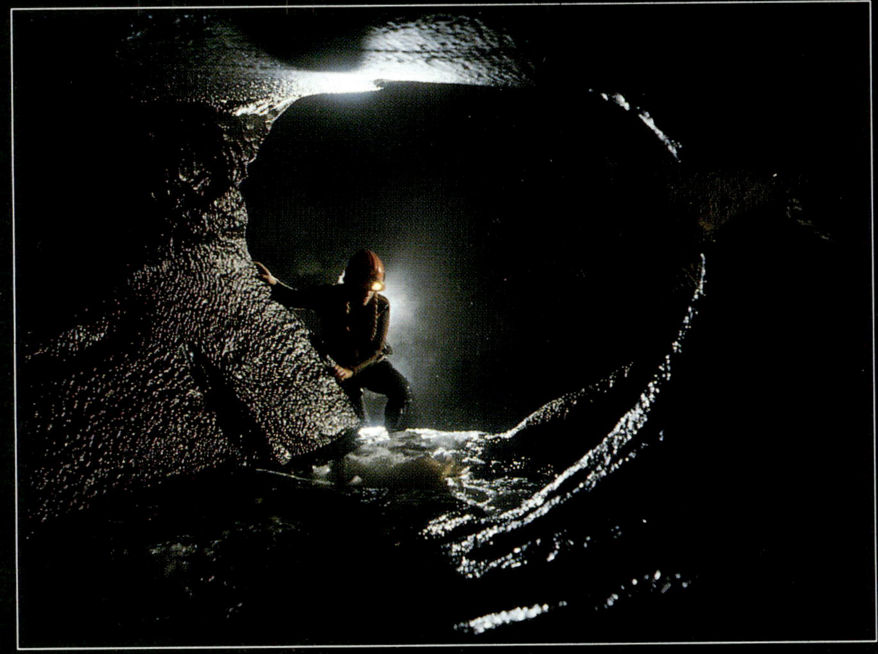

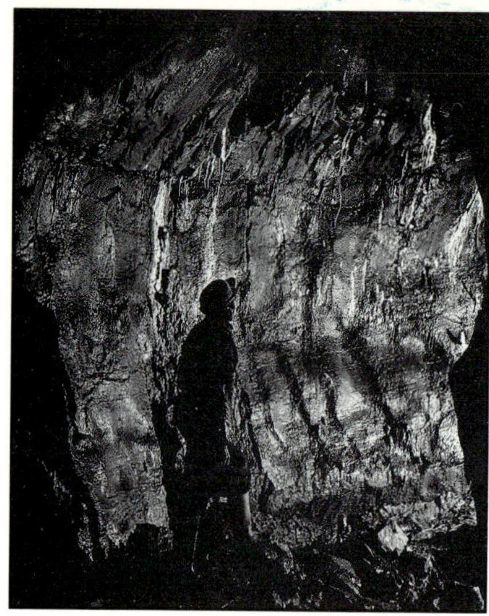

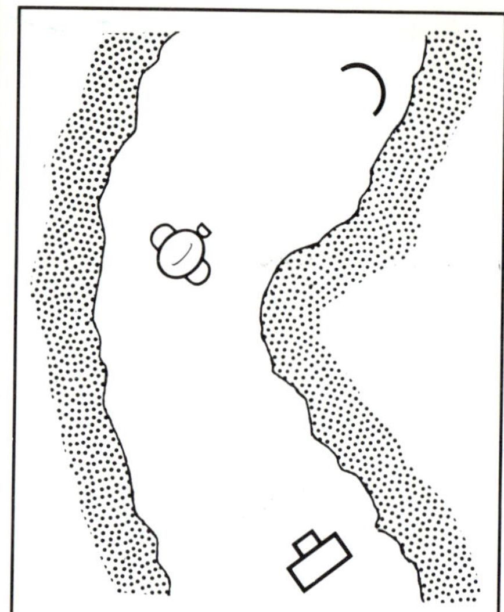

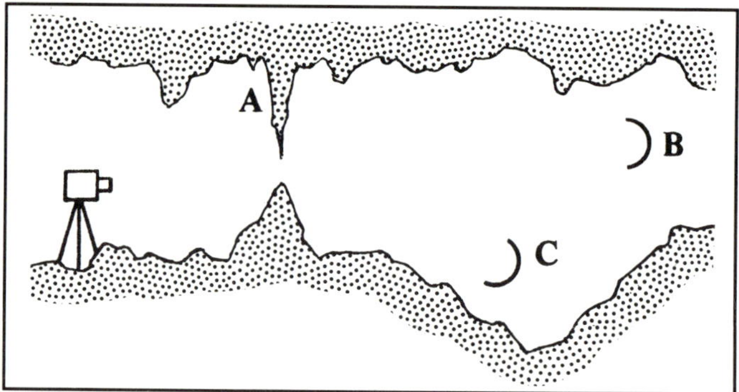

Placing Flashguns

For back or side lighting the flashgun has to be hidden from the camera. For thinner subjects such as stalactites (A) this may be impossible to obtain. Flash position B would be in view, but much the same effect can be produced by placing the flash in a hollow (C). By placing it round the corner of a passage, as in ***Ogof Ffynnon Ddu*** *(B4), adds relief and texture to rock.*

clean and polished can make a difference of one stop to the aperture, eg, from f4 to f5.6. If high power or a wide spread of light is required, use a bulb.

Usually, a reflector on a bulb gun gives a wide and relatively diffuse light (since the reflector is usually a large one) that spreads over a little under 180°. Electronic flashguns use a narrower beam of about 90°, which is not enough to cover the full field of view of a wide angle 28mm lens. In addition, when using a light to show the shape of a passage a bulb has enough spread to hit all the walls. Being more directional the flash from an electronic gun has more of a tendency to disappear along the passage, very little hitting the walls at all.

Bulbs do have disadvantages. Apart from expense and bulk they are slow to reload when compared to the recharge time of an electronic flash. The best solution overall is to have both types available, using whichever one is most suited to the picture being taken. For example, a caver standing in a passage is asked to fire a flashgun away from the camera, silhouetting himself. If he fires a bulb he will show up both the passage and himself, whilst the electronic flash does not. At most, light from the electronic gun scatters on moisture in the air and shows up the caver but does not always also have the spread to illuminate the walls. On the other hand, side lighting scallops on a wall to show relief is best done with electronic flash. There would be no advantage in using a bulb, which is more expensive.

The final characteristic of light is its duration. A bulb has a slow build up of light intensity, which peaks and then tails off, the whole process taking about 1/30th of a second, a relatively slow time. Electronic flashes have a shorter duration, from around 1/1,000th to 1/20,000th of a second.

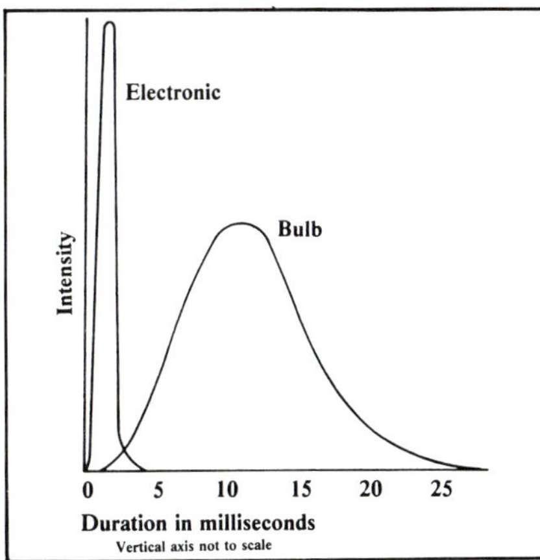

Flash Characteristics

An electronic flash produces a very short duration burst of light whilst a bulb is slow to build up and fall off. This difference produces difficulties in producing slave units which will be fired by the slow reaction time of a bulb rather than the sudden change in intensity of an electronic gun, whilst remaining unaffected by caplamps. Using 'B' or 'X' at 1/30th second or slower the total light output of a bulb may be used.

It is for this reason that cameras need to synchronise at speeds of 1/30th of a second or slower for caving use, for otherwise part of the light output of a bulb would be lost. It also explains why some slave units will not be triggered by a bulb. The better kind of slaves react to fast changes in illumination, and the gradual peaking of a bulb flash is too slow for them to consistently detect. A slave sensitive enough to be triggered by a slowly reacting bulb would be unstable and could easily be set off by glancing light from a caplamp.

These different durations can be used to good effect when lighting cave interiors. Since the flash duration effectively takes the picture, even when the camera shutter is used in synchronisation with slave units, use of an electronic flash will 'freeze' motion whilst bulbs will allow it to blur. Water and spray falling through the air can be stopped by the action of the electronic flash. The same subject takes on a feeling of fluidity with a bulb, water droplets streaking out into long lines. If a crisp action picture of a caver in motion is needed, use an electronic flash. For impressions of motion, use bulbs to allow blurring. Both types have their uses; decide what you wish the picture to look like and use them accordingly.

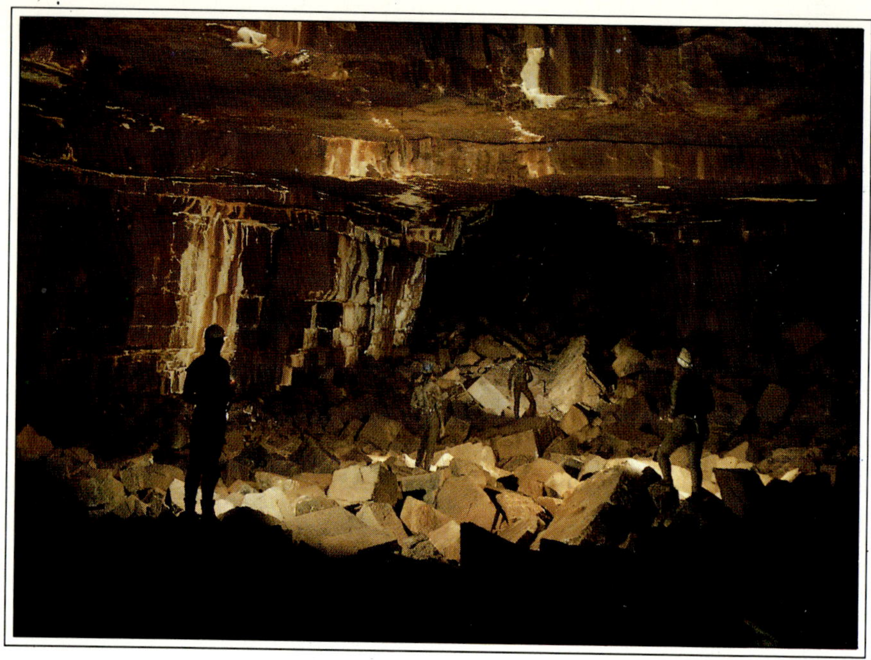

Ogof Ffynnon Ddu. *Each caver fires a flash at roughly equal distances from each other, producing even illumination.*

Determining The Aperture

Once you have decided what to take a picture of, found the best place for the camera position, decided upon the type of light to be used and placed the flashgun, there is one last factor to determine before the button can be pressed. The aperture.

A camera aperture controls the amount of light that is allowed through the lens to reach the film, and is measured in 'f ' stops. The bigger the number, the smaller the aperture and the more light is needed for a correct exposure since only a portion of that which is produced will be allowed through the lens. Changing from one 'f ' stop to the next will either halve or double the light reaching the film. Thus, a change from f5.6 to f8 uses a smaller aperture and halves the light that is allowed through. The benefit of a small aperture is in depth of field; more of both foreground and background is in focus with smaller 'f ' stops. There is always a trade off in trying to produce enough light to permit a small aperture to gain this depth of field.

Rather than being a mysterious, arcane art, determination of the correct aperture to use for any given flashgun - either electronic or bulb - is quite straightforward. As light leaves the flashgun it spreads out. The greater the distance it has to travel, the less there is to hit the subject, and doubling the distance involved will in fact quarter the light reaching the subject. Thus, it is always the flash-to-subject distance that is important, never the camera-to-subject. The latter can be ignored totally, apart from focussing of course.

To determine the aperture use the guide number of the flashgun or bulb. If the guide number is divided by the distance from flash to subject, the number obtained is the aperture. Ensure that you estimate your distances in metres if the guide number was worked out using these, feet if the guide number was in feet. Older flashbulbs usually used guide numbers in feet, but modern guides are always worked out using metres. In either case;

$$\textbf{Guide Number} = \textbf{Distance} \times \textbf{Aperture.}$$

$$\textbf{Aperture} = \frac{\textbf{Guide Number}}{\textbf{Distance}}$$

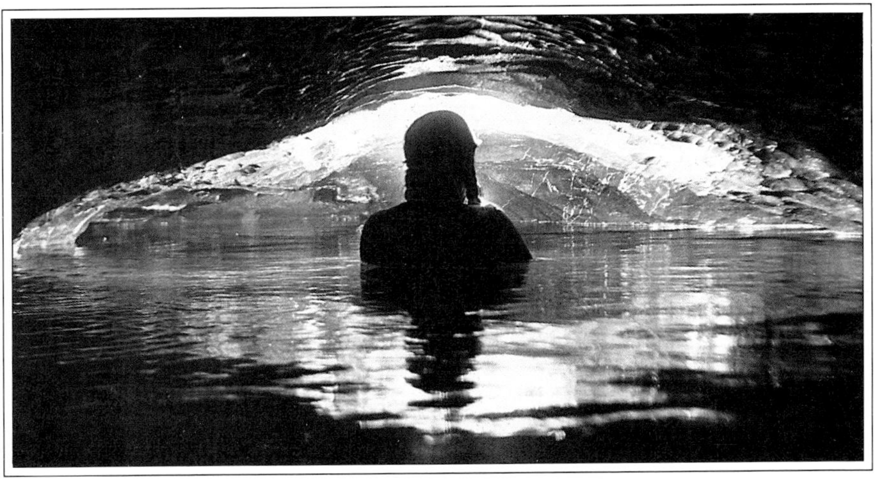

Porth yr Ogof. *One of the simplest techniques to use. The camera is set on 'B', and the caver manually fires a flash, producing a silhouette and showing the passage shape.*

Suppose, for example, that with 100 ISO film a flash has a guide number of 30 in metres. 30 is the important number. The subject of the picture is 5 metres away. 30/5 equals 6. You should therefore set f6. Look on your lens; there is no such number. However, intermediate settings can be used so use a position between f5.6 and f8, or set the next closest; f5.6.

If you are using 200 ISO film rather than 100 ISO, this is twice as sensitive, and you would use f8 instead of f5.6. Likewise, use f4 with 50 ISO. Every time an ISO is doubled or halved the aperture changes by one stop.

If you prefer working in feet, use a guide number determined using feet. This is usually in the region of 100. It is fairly easy to work out with the above formula, even if it is not quoted by the manufacturer: there will usually be a chart of guide numbers and aperture/ISO combinations on the back of the flashgun or bulb packet. To alter a guide number quoted in metres to one in feet (if you prefer working in feet) multiply by 3.3.

The main difficulty is that these methods of determining the aperture are theoretical. They work well with reasonably reflective subjects such as stalactites or a caver's face or oversuit, but on dark rock or mud less light is reflected than would be expected. Likewise, white calcite reflects more. With experience you will be able to judge what situations will not give good results when using guide numbers, and can change the aperture accordingly. For instance, mud can require the aperture to be opened up one or two stops to retain detail.

Leaving the aperture as the guide number suggests will give a 'correct' exposure, but not necessarily a pleasing one or the one you desire. The manufacturer may not

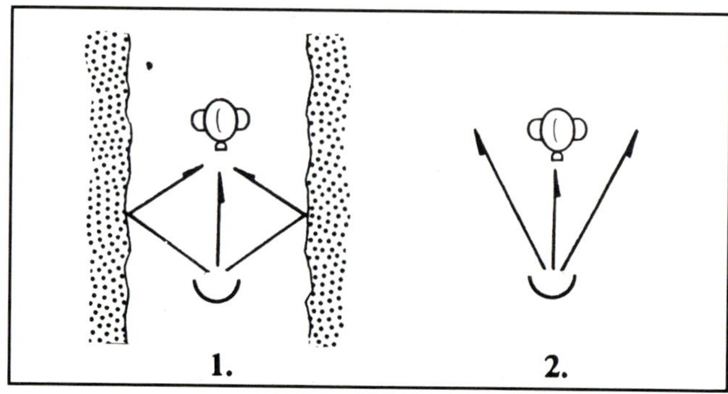

Modifying Guide Numbers

In confined situations (1), light will be reflected onto the subject from the walls, as in ***Upper Flood Swallet*** *(E8, E4). The original manufacture's guide number may be accurate in this case, unlike (2) where no added light is reflected from the side. This will require a different guide number, modified from the original by experience.*

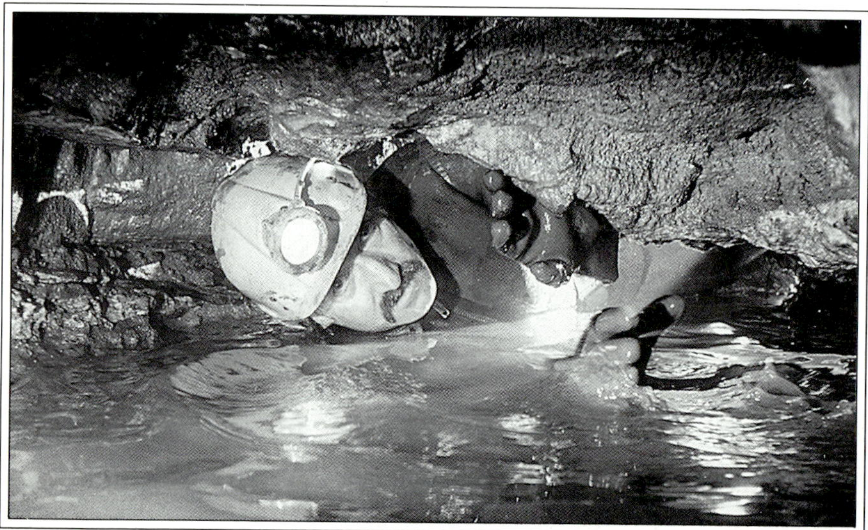

have quoted a realistic value, and it will not be suited to caving conditions. Because of this you will need to experiment a little. Bracket the exposure - take the same picture with a variation of apertures - in case your judgement is wrong. The results will indicate a more realistic guide number for future uses, and help you gain experience. You will probably find that your theoretical guide number will be halved at least for practical use underground. Bracketing exposures may use up more film, but it makes it certain you will obtain a correctly exposed picture that suits the effect you want.

Altering the theoretical exposure can be dangerous in some situations. Most articles on cave photography recommend that the aperture is opened up by at least one or two stops. This general guide will be true for most situations underground, but not all. You should be aware of those situations in which the original, theoretical, aperture will be accurate. In these cases using your modified aperture will usually result in over exposure.

These situations arise when there is a reflective subject being photographed, either filling the frame or only a part of it. For example, if light is directed onto a reflective subject such as a face this will easily be overexposed if you have previously opened the aperture by a stop. Take care if there is a dark area of rock with a caver in front. There is a temptation of using a larger aperture to gain detail in the limestone, but if this is done the caver will be burned out, a washed-out white face the result and the picture ruined.

Thus, it is a fallacy that the aperture must be opened up by an equal amount in all situations. If a lot of light can be reflected from walls onto the subject, eg. in a confined crawl or passage, the situation is once more similar to that used by the manufacturer when the original guide number was computed. Experience will soon indicate when you should use your modified guide number and open up the aperture by the amount determined in your experiments, and when to use the original one quoted on the flashgun. If in doubt, photograph the same picture at both settings. This costs more in film, but little extra in time and ensures at least one correct exposure.

One good method of developing a standard technique is to use the guide number and practical experimentation to get a perfectly exposed picture, and note the distance and aperture you used. For example, 15ft at f5.6 with 200 ASA film produces a perfectly exposed photograph. Leave the aperture on f5.6, and always place your flashgun at 15ft distance from the subject. Working in this way with a standard set up lessens the number of mistakes that you will initially make underground. The final information of distance and aperture used with that flashgun can then be written on it for future reference, although some occasions such as those detailed above may necessitate on-the-spot alterations.

Practice using one flash, and become conversant with the results you can obtain before trying to become too adventurous with other effects. There are many fine, dramatic, atmospheric pictures that can be taken with this most basic of equipment. It is not necessarily the photographer with the greatest number of flashguns and apparatus that produces the best pictures; technique, imagination and originality have much more power and effect.

4
MULTIPLE FLASH

Whilst lighting pictures with a single flashgun is quick and highly effective, and certainly suitable for use on sporting trips or to document digs or work such as surveying, it is also limiting. When larger areas have to be photographed, or for special effects, multiple flashes are required.

Using The 'B' Setting

Producing multiple flashes need not entail the use of a second flashgun. If, for example, a tripod or ball and socket head on an ammunition box is in use and the shutter is set on 'B', the same flashgun can be set off several times, each flash adding more light to the picture. This could be from the same place, enabling a brighter flash to be built up, or from different areas so that the photograph is 'painted in', and built up like pieces of a jigsaw.

It is important that nothing being photographed is allowed to move during the exposure, or double images will arise. For example, a picture is taken of a caver using two flashes to illuminate him. If he moves between the two, even slightly, there will be a ghost image with two heads, and so on. If someone using a flashgun has to move to a new position they must either do so in the dark, without the use of their caplamps, or the lens has to be covered by the photographer. The simplest method is to drape a lens cloth over the lens, allow the 'flasher' to move using his caplamp to see by, then remove the cloth when his lamp is off once more. A lens cap can also be used, but there is then a chance of moving the camera

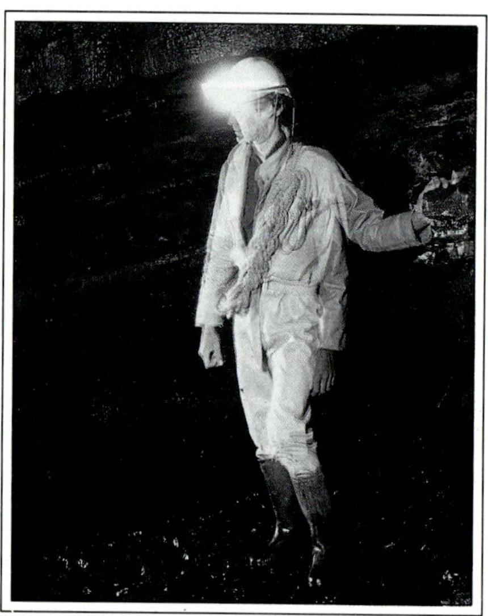

Ogof Ffynnon Ddu. *E2, E7. Movement of a caver between flashes whilst the camera is on 'B' produces a double image.*

whilst it is fitted or removed. Tripods used in caves are unlikely to be of the sturdiest variety due to the size problems of carrying them, and this is a real danger.

Instil into everybody involved the fact that they mustn't move unless told that they can. Inevitably someone will turn round after the first flash has fired with an 'OK?', or will switch on their lamps just before the cable release is pressed to end the shot. It also helps, if everybody including yourself is involved in firing flashguns, to leave a weak light some distance behind the tripod so that it can be found again without too much difficulty. Kicking over the camera whilst attempting to locate the cable release does not lead to a good picture!

Because of the difficulty in keeping the camera still between separate flashes it is not possible to use a hand held camera on 'B', since inevitably the camera itself will move even if the subject is stationary. The choice when using multiple flash is either a camera mounted on a tripod, or slave units. The latter, once again, permits much greater flexibility in use, and speed. However, the basic principles involved in multiple flash remain the same for either system.

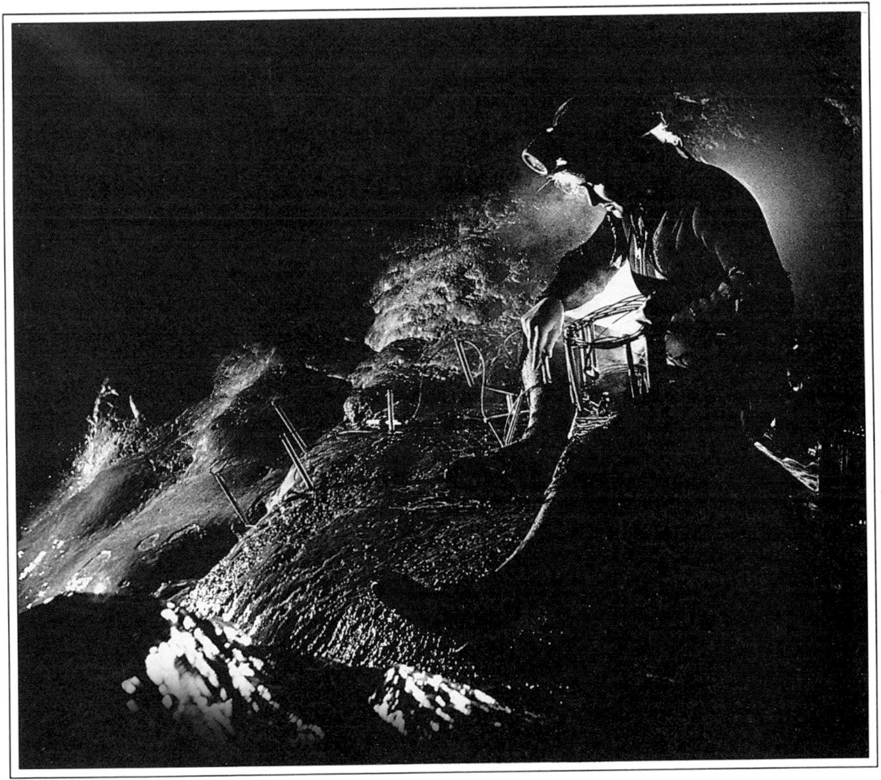

Lower Long Churn. *The restricted angle of illumination of electronic flash at E5 and E7, fired by infra red slave, has retained the dark surroundings and avoided overlighting the picture.*

Placing Flashguns

Placement of the flashguns is very important for these techniques if a balanced photograph is to be the result. The same basic positions for lights are available as before; front, side and back light. The same rules apply as for single flash; never place a flash too close to the camera.

There are three main occasions when more than one flash is required. Firstly, several flashes might be needed from one place to build up added power, or to aim them in slightly different directions to give a wider spread of light. This would usually be applicable with electronic flash, for example to light a large formation from a single position when one flash could be fired at the base, another at the top, and so on.

Secondly, there is the classic effect produced by a string of cavers spread out down a long straight passage, receding into the distance. Another is a photograph of a large chamber, where cavers fire flashguns from various places around its circumference to light the walls. These sort of photographs are a lot easier to produce than they might seem at first, and if the principles of using single flash are fully understood, and your experiences have taught you the best exposures to use with your flashguns, there should be little difficulty.

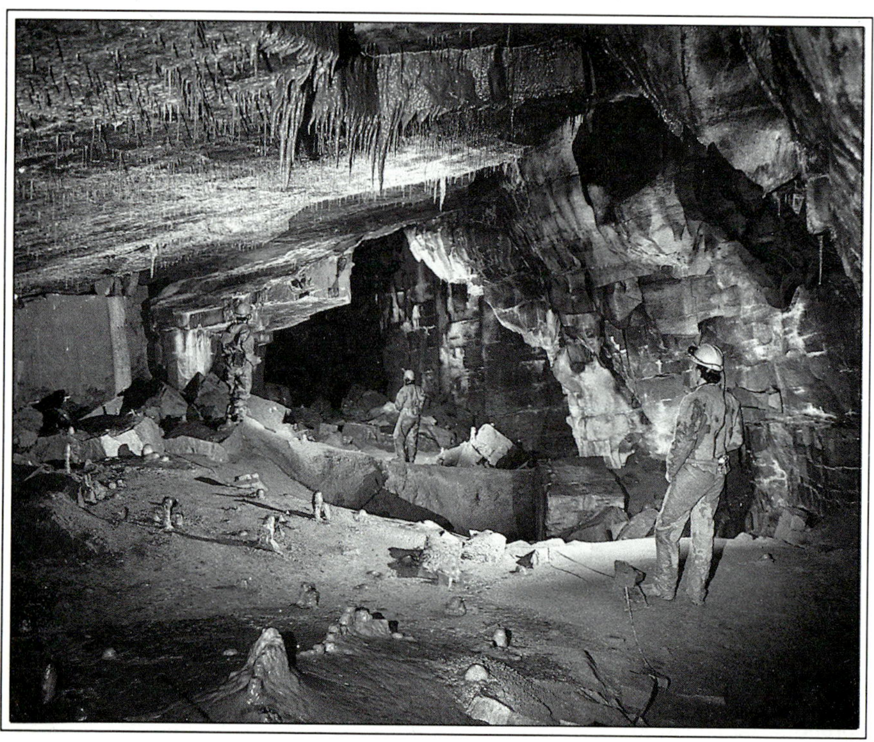

***Ogof Ffynnon Ddu**. Each caver fires a flash at roughly equal distances from each other, producing even illumination.*

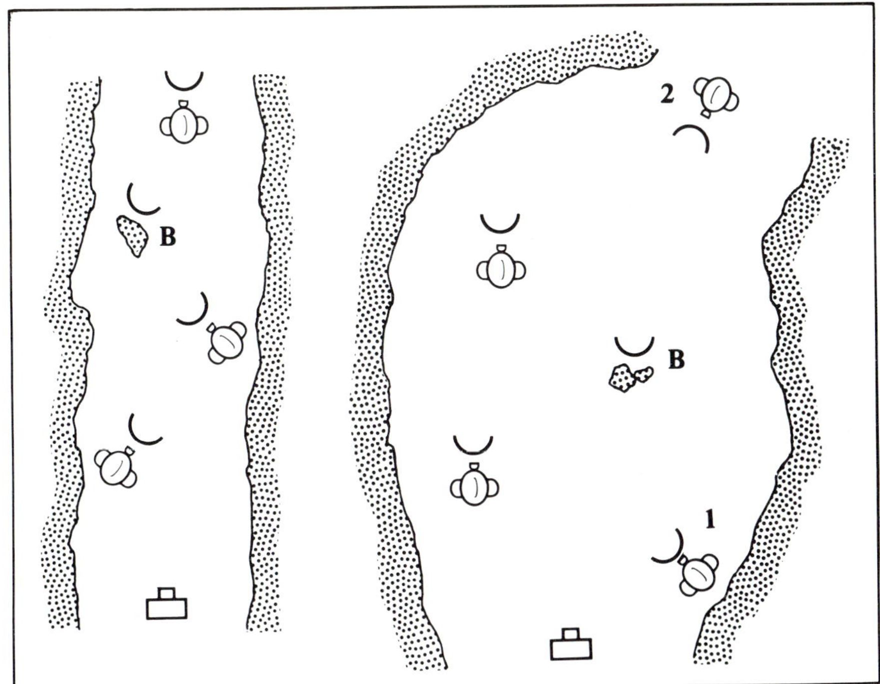

Multiple Lighting Positions

When multiple flash is used, whether in a passage or large chamber, flashguns should be kept roughly equidistant from each other to retain even illumination. Hiding some lights behind boulders (B) can help to break up a too-regular composition. Flashgun 1 adds foreground detail without being in the picture itself. Light at position 2 provides some backlight, and is hidden from the camera position by the boulders.

The usual system is to give every caver a flashgun, either fired by slaves or manually by the caver pressing a test button. The further slave units may be well out of range of the camera flash, but this will not matter since the first flash triggers the slave, which in turn triggers the next, and so on. Using slaves, it is not even necessary to have a caver holding them, and electronic flashguns can be left switched on to recharge and be ready to fire for subsequent shots. In this way lights can be hidden behind rocks within the picture area.

When firing guns manually with the camera on a tripod the shutter is locked open on 'B'. A signal is then given, which could be the first flash being fired, or a whistle. This is far more effective than a shout. Sound becomes muffled down a passage, and all too often when a caver is asked if he is ready a flash results before the shutter is opened. "Oh, sorry," is the reply. "I thought you said you were ready." A prearranged signal, whatever it is, must be concise, specific, and not prone to be misunderstood. Photographs using multiple flash take time to set up, and cost a great deal of effort. Wasting both time and effort due to a lack of organisation is unwarranted.

With several cavers strung out down a passage, each should be illuminated by the one behind. The same principle may hold true for chambers, or you may decide to aim lights onto areas of wall or roof. It is important to light at least one figure in these photographs, or else the scale of the place is lost. Some lights might be hidden behind boulders or around corners. Breaking up a regular arrangement of people adds to the interest of a photograph, whilst keeping flashes at equal distances retains an even spread of light.

The need to obtain even lighting is usually important, something which is difficult if there are not enough flashguns in use. Too few flashguns create patches of light, each unconnected with the next, beside each caver. If too many lights are used an overlit scene lacking depth or atmosphere results. Caves, being dark places, need areas of black left in the picture or else the effect looks unnatural.

Obtaining Even Lighting

To get even lighting several flashguns are preferable to a few. The principle is to use a number of light sources that can be spread out, and give better coverage, rather than one overpowering flash which overexposes the foreground and underexposes the background.

Determining the exposure to use with multiple flash is straightforward if tackled in the right way. Using a flash on its own, the guide number determines the aperture to use. One suggested photographic technique is to mark each flashgun with the correct working distance and aperture for use. Thus, every time a picture is to be taken of a similar nature (like a caver in a passage or by a formation) the flash is placed the same distance away, and the aperture kept constant. If all the flashguns have been marked with distances that give the same aperture the use of multiple flash is very straightforward. There are numerous advantages to using this system.

For example, if all your flashguns give a correct exposure at 20ft at f5.6 and they are all placed at 20ft distance from the separate areas they are illuminating the exposure will still be correct at f5.6, no matter how many flashguns are actually in

Obtaining Even Lighting

A photograph of the caver and stalagmites (S) can be lit using a flashgun at A. However, the caver is closer to the flash than the stalagmites and if he is correctly illuminated the formations will be underexposed. A better lighting position is (B), roughly equidistant from each subject. Lighting is even, and both will be correctly exposed. When more than one subject is to be lit either use two flashguns or choose an intermediate lighting position between them.

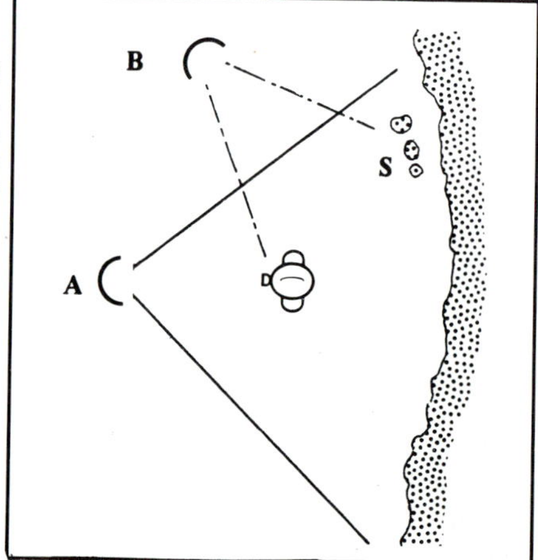

use. Large chambers or long passages can be easily and evenly illuminated in this way. Keeping cavers that are firing flashguns at roughly equal distances from each other therefore simplifies exposure problems enormously.

Since you cannot change the aperture on the camera for each individual flash, you must change the distance each gun is fired from to suit the aperture you have chosen. If you have different flashguns in use, place each one at its correct distance. The guide number formula can be worked to give distance instead of aperture if you do not normally work in this way;

$$\textbf{Distance} = \frac{\textbf{Guide Number}}{\textbf{Aperture}}$$

Thus, suppose one of your flashguns has a guide number of 40 for the film in use, far more powerful than the rest which have guide numbers of 30. You are to use an aperture of f4 at 8 metres, this being the aperture and distance you usually use with the weaker guns. The powerful gun must be placed at a distance of 40/4 = 10 metres to give the same level of illumination.

This is great for a general guide, but never forget that a guide is all that it is and it will still not replace experience in recognising difficulties before they occur rather than when you are back home with the processed film. The same comments concerning corrections and modifications to guide numbers, detailed in section 3, apply just as much to multiple flash situations.

Using more than one flashgun does enable some problems to be solved, though. For example, a caver standing some distance in front of a dark rock wall is to be photographed. A single flash from the front will either overexpose the caver, or leave the background too dark. The front flash, if used, must give a correct exposure to the caver, which may mean using an unmodified guide number. A second flash can be placed to illuminate the rock and balance the lighting.

Using this technique you should not deliberately place two guns to illuminate the same area. Some light spilling over from one area to the next is impossible to avoid, but it will not materially affect the picture. However, exposure problems occur if two front lights combine their effects to any degree, for example doubling the illumination in just part of the scene. Overexposure in this area will be the result.

Adding Backlighting

Another technique of using extra lights is to place one directly behind the subject for backlighting. This extra light adds highlights to walls and roof, and gives rim-lit figures. Used in addition to side lighting the effect is dramatic, and lifts even an ordinary photograph into an interesting, exciting one. If light is required on the surrounding cave passage or generally across water surfaces, use a bulb both for power and spread of light. If it is only required on the caver or formation, use an electronic flash. In either case, the power of the flash and the distance it is placed at is not critical; anywhere about ten feet behind the subject is suitable. With experience you will be able to modify this distance to suit yourself.

With the flash being directed towards the camera the main effect is the addition of pure white highlights to ceiling, floor and walls. Mid tones - greys - are controlled by side or front lighting, not backlighting. Varying the backlight/subject distance produces different forms of highlights, for example making them larger or spread

Bridge Cave. *A single flash E1 produces detail, but a poor photograph. The effects of adding a flash at E5 and then moving E1 to E3 illustrate the production of contrast and backlighting.*

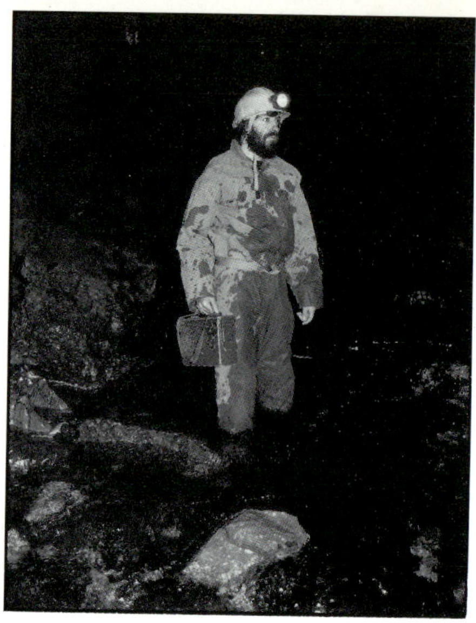

over a different area. Effectively, the backlight can be ignored when calculating the exposure to use. This will be determined by the side or front light alone, although too powerful a backlight (or one used too close) will burn out areas of the picture.

For the precise placing of a backlight you will probably be dependant upon another caver. It would be a rare cave that has a convenient ledge just in the right place. An accurate line up of flash, subject and camera is crucial so that the camera falls into the shadow area that is produced. This can be checked for effect by turning off your own caplamp and seeing the effect from your assistant's helmet light. If the flash is held close to this position when it is fired its effect can be accurately judged.

To enable your assistant to line up the flash it helps a great deal if your own light is left on dip; when you are out of his sight he knows his flash is in the right place. Accurate line up is the key to success, and is much easier to accomplish by moving the backlight; an assistant that understands what is required and can do this without constant instructions is a great asset. This is one situation which can be simulated on the surface beforehand so that the caver placing the backlight knows exactly how to produce the effect you wish to obtain. Trying to instruct someone in the cave can take time, especially if there is running water to mask voices and make communication difficult.

To completely hide one person behind another is difficult. The flash should be held slightly in front of the body, especially using bulbs with their wide angle of illumination. Any stray light does not then hit the person holding the flash and he blends into darkness. Even if arms or legs protrude into the picture area they won't be seen.

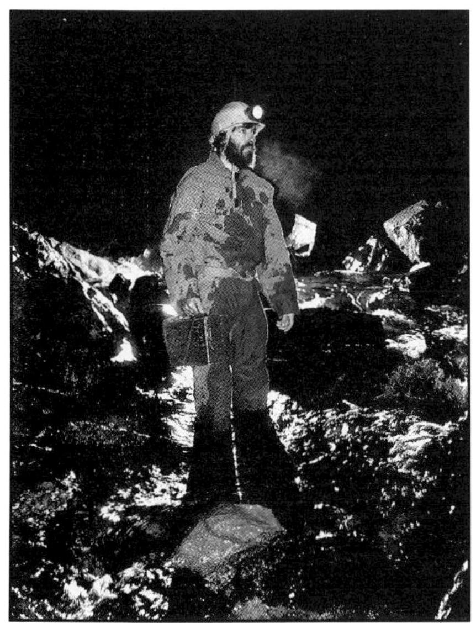 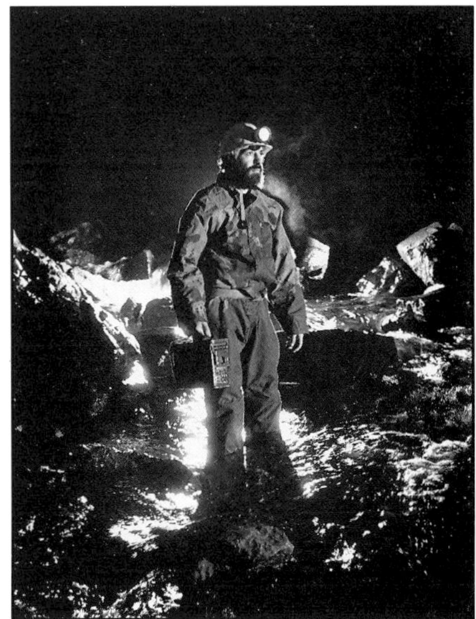

Bulb And Electronic Flash Combinations

Using bulbs together with electronic flash produces a further possibility. The difference in the angle of illumination of each can be used to good effect, for example when using a bulb for backlight and an electronic flashgun for side or front light. The former is powerful, and adds rimlighting and drama. The latter is directional, and used with care will permit a very specific part of the picture to be lit, leaving the rest to flow into darkness.

This is one occasion when flashes can be triggered by slave units to fire in synchronisation with the electronic flash being used with 'computer' sensor in operation rather than having to be put on manual. Normally, if two guns have sensors working at the same time they pick up light from each other and the sensor mechanisms of both of them are fooled. The picture is underexposed as a result. Whenever two electronic guns are used they must both be set to manual to avoid this interference. There is one exception. If the front flash is electronic and is computer controlled, it's short flash duration finishes before a bulb has even properly begun to emit light. Thus, the two do not interfere with each other, and can be used in combination. Working in such a way gives good control of lighting and accurate rendition of flesh-tones, although the general limitations of sensors must be born in mind.

It is always wise to restrict the effects of lights and keep any arrangement as simple as possible. There is a danger of wanting to use too many flashguns just because they happen to be available (and working!) on that particular occasion. A simple arrangement is much more likely to be effective than a complex one, and if the intention is to produce more than a straightforward record picture limit the number of flashes involved, or use them with discretion so as not to confuse the viewer.

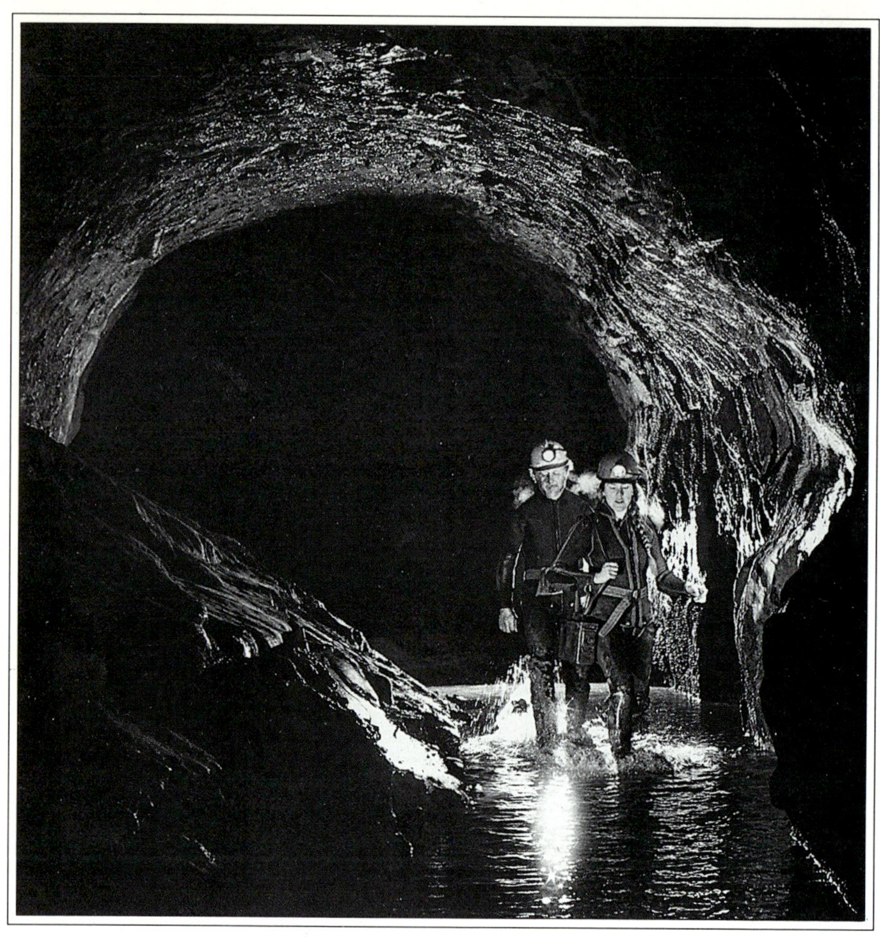

Sleets Gill. *The combined effects of electronic and bulb flash are shown here. Two electronic flashes were concealed each side of the passage at E2 and E8. Their directional flash lit the figures but not the foreground. B5, with a wide spread of light, has shown up the passage shape.*

The 'Father of Speleology', E.A. Martel, considered that light should only ever be used from one source and categorically banned flashes from within the picture area. He felt that too many lights interfered with the 'correct' rendition of the scene. In some ways, whilst his rigid rules concerning lighting placement have not stood the test of time, he was correct. The production of a simple arrangement of light (or one that looks simple in the final picture) is the best way to produce an effective picture.

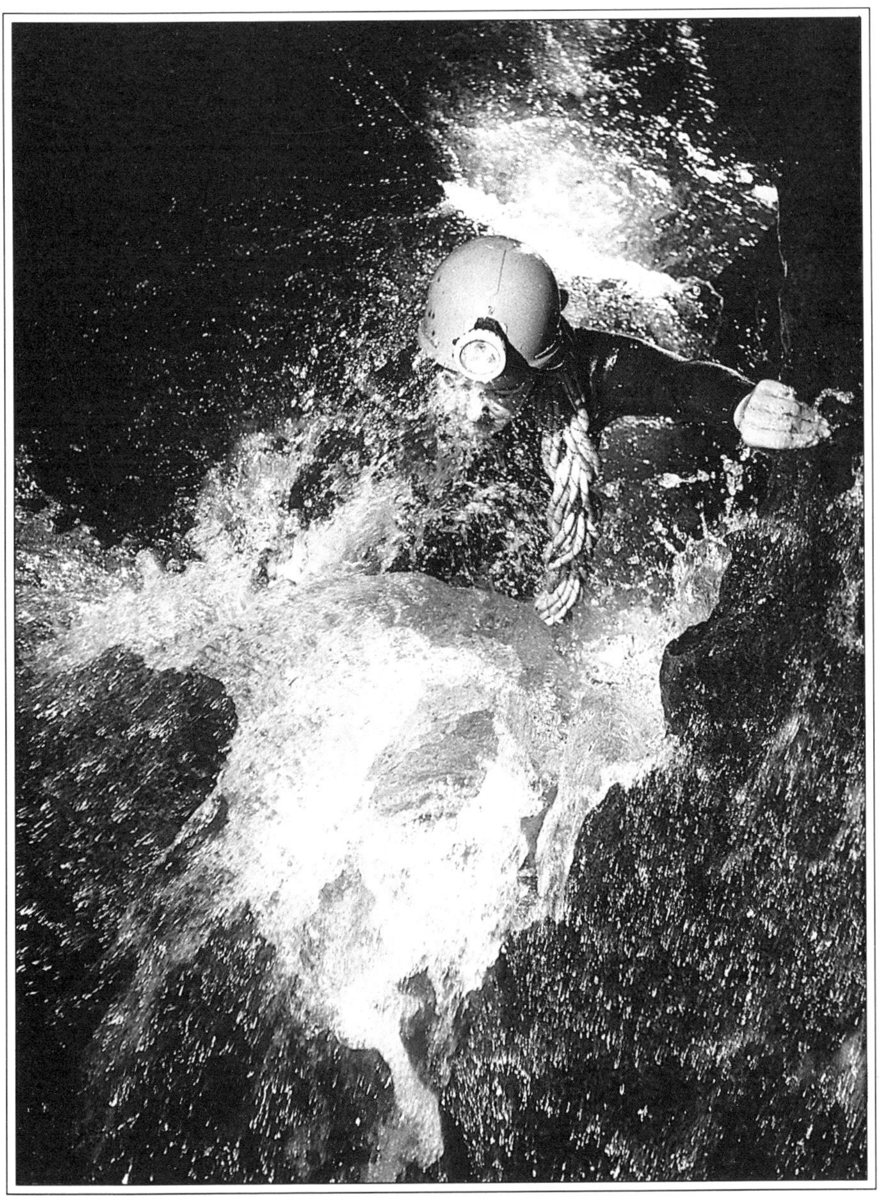

Ogof Ffynnon Ddu. *E8 and E5 have been placed at the correct distances from the subject to provide even lighting both in front and behind.*

CONCLUSION

It will be obvious by now that a cave photographer is very dependent upon the aid given to him by his friends, both in posing to add scale, carrying equipment, and in holding flashguns. It is worth considering what they gain from the production of your pictures both during and after the trip, and making sure that they are still willing to come and help again on another occasion. In short, keeping them happy will help you in the future. As a bonus, you are likely to find your photographs much improved due to their added involvement. Contributions from other members of the team can be invaluable, an aspect that is often ignored.

To ensure things run smoothly a well planned trip is the first requirement. Choose your locations with care, and have an idea of what you want before you even leave the house. Add other pictures to the set if you see them when in the cave, but try to have at least a few planned out beforehand. This alone will help give the whole trip an objective.

Once you begin to take the picture, try to involve everybody so that no-one is left to stand around and get cold and bored. For this reason it is perhaps best to limit your party to three or four, unless you specifically need more. With four cavers, for example, one can act as a model whilst two operate flashguns and you work the camera. Keep people active, or tell them they can go and explore or look around if they are not needed for a while. Keep them informed rather than ignored.

Your instructions should be as precise as possible. Decide exactly where you want each flash fired. Give concise instructions about when to fire the flash. Rather than tell the model to 'stand over there' it is often best to go with them and stand exactly how you want them to be; show them, don't tell them. It is the person in a picture of this sort that will produce a winning photograph, or unwittingly cause its failure. A poor pose will ruin an otherwise perfectly executed and properly exposed photograph. An expression of boredom destroys the most carefully planned picture. All in all, a good model that can follow directions whilst looking relaxed and natural is worth his (or her) weight in gold.

For the same reasons, explain what you are trying to do in each picture. Involving others can lead to further ideas being produced by them. If they are interested and a part of the production they are less likely to stand about and get cold and fed up. Persuading someone to lie down in freezing water for a photograph is one thing, but to do so and then waste time organising the flashguns is another. If you can train a team of helpers who can frequently cave with you the whole process becomes faster, efficient, and more enjoyable for everyone involved.

After the trip you will have a set of prints or slides to examine. Keep the interest of others by making sure they have some copies. It is a small price to pay for their continued aid, especially since the pictures couldn't be produced without them.

Easgill Caverns. *E8, hidden amongst the stalagmites, has illuminated the caver. B6 lights the straws in Easter Grotto. The use of infra red rather than visible light slaves has permitted synchronisation without loss of a black foreground.*

Ogof Ffynnon Ddu. *The usefulness of both electronic and bulb flash is shown in Selenite Tunnel. E1 has lit the figure, but is directional enough to leave the edges dark. B5 has a spread of 180°, giving both backlight to the caver and showing the passage shape.*

You should also carefully study the effects you have obtained. Are they just what you expected to produce? Did the equipment work as it should, and what could you make or modify to avoid the same problem next time? Would the light be better further to the left? Did you break the cardinal rule and place a flash too close to the lens and produce a flat, boring, low contrast photograph? Would a bulb instead of an electronic gun have given more spread of light and aided the composition? Is the exposure correct?

Run over a check list that includes technical details such as exposure, composition including the lighting angles and effects they produce, and the ability of the model in the picture. Admittedly, some cavers can never pose successfully, but before you put all the blame on them were your own instructions precise enough? Did you, in fact, know what you wanted with sufficient detail to explain the pose to them? If you are critical of your efforts, whatever the reasons for failure, then you will improve the next time. A realistic analysis of your successes and failures is very important. Learn from the mistakes that you will inevitably make, until you are able to produce just the picture you want.

But, above all, enjoy its production. It's only if you have had some fun as well as obtaining a stunning photograph that all the discomfort, conning friends into helping you (against their better judgement), crawling through sticky mud, and dragging a heavy box filled with expensive equipment, becomes worthwhile.

It would be too much to believe that everything on a cave photography trip works just as expected all the time. Flashguns fail, cameras jam, untrained helpers move at just the wrong moment. If taking pictures underground is arguably the hardest form of photography, then the production of a successful print or slide is worth all the frustration and effort involved, and is something to be proud of. That fact is worth remembering the next time you happen to be underground, and nothing - but nothing - will go right!

***Poulnagollum Pot**. The front light is hidden behind a boulder, below the camera, to retain a dark surround. E1, B6.*

Index

Ammunition Box 36-37
Analysis of results 67
Angle of illumination 45, 48
Aperture 14, 50-53
ASA 23

B setting 7, 23, 40-42, 54-55, 57
Backlight 59-60
Ball and socket head 37
Battery 18, 30-31, 34
BDH containers 37

Cable release 7, 23
Camera 6, 10-13, 26-27
Camera, choice 6
Camera, protection of 26-27
Camera, SLR 12-13
Camera, underwater 10, 11
Cleaning 38
Close up 12
Computer flash sensor 15-17
Condensation 44
Contrast 23

Double images 54
Duration of flash 49

Film 23-24
Film, chromogenic 24
Filters 27
Flashbulb 14, 18, 30-32, 34, 45, 61
Flash, duration of 40, 49
Flash, power of 15
Flashguns, bulb 18, 30-32, 34
Flashguns, electronic 14-17, 27-28, 61
Flash synchronisation 7, 10, 15, 28

Guide number 32, 51-53, 59

Hot shoe 7

Infra red 21, 35
Insurance 38
ISO 23, 24

Lens 7, 12-14
Lens, focal length 13
Lens, zoom 13
Light meter 10

Mines 10
Models 64
Modifications to flashguns 28
Multiple flash 54-61

Packing equipment 38

Rangefinder 11
Red eye 44
Reflector 48

Sensor 15-17
Shutter speed 7, 40
Silhouettes 40, 45
Silica gel 37
Slave unit 15, 18-19, 21 35, 42

Synchronisation of flash 7, 10, 15, 28

Tripod 7, 21, 23, 37
Tripod, choice of 21, 23
Tripod bush 7

Viewfinder 7